I LOVE HORSES

ALSO BY STEVEN D. PRICE

I LOVE HORSES

Edited and with an Introduction by
STEVEN D. PRICE

Photographs Edited by
Autumn Michels and Madison Torre

LYONS
PRESS

Essex, Connecticut

An imprint of Globe Pequot, the trade division of
The Rowman & Littlefield Publishing Group, Inc.
4501 Forbes Blvd., Ste. 200
Lanham, MD 20706
www.rowman.com

Distributed by NATIONAL BOOK NETWORK

British Library Cataloguing in Publication Information available

Library of Congress Cataloging-in-Publication Data
Names: Price, Steven D., editor.
Title: I love horses / edited and with an Introduction by Steven D. Price ;
    photographs edited by Autumn Michels and Madison Torre
Description: Essex, Connecticut : Lyons Press, [2024] | Summary: "All the
    most evocative words ever written or spoken about horse, together with
    photographs of this magnificent animal"— Provided by publisher.
Identifiers: LCCN 2024006472 (print) | LCCN 2024006473 (ebook) | ISBN
    9781493086870 (paperback) | ISBN 9781493086887 (epub)
Subjects: LCSH: Horses—Pictorial works. | Horses—Miscellanea. |
    Horses—Quotations, maxims, etc.
Classification: LCC SF303 .I46 2024 (print) | LCC SF303 (ebook) | DDC
    779.32—dc23/eng/20240424
LC record available at https://lccn.loc.gov/2024006472
LC ebook record available at https://lccn.loc.gov/2024006473

♾™ The paper used in this publication meets the minimum requirements
of American National Standard for Information Sciences—Permanence of
Paper for Printed Library Materials, ANSI/NISO Z39.48-1992.

Yet when all the books have been read and reread, it boils down to the horse, his human companion, and what goes on between them.

—WALTER FARLEY, AUTHOR OF THE BLACK STALLION SERIES, QUOTED IN *THE RANDOM HOUSE BOOK OF HORSES AND HORSEMANSHIP* BY PAULA RODENAS

By reading, riding and meditating, great results may be obtained, if there is true feeling for the horse and provided the rider's seat is good.

—NUNO OLIVEIRA, *REFLECTIONS ON EQUESTRIAN ART*

CONTENTS

■ ■ ■ ■ ■ ■ ■ ■ ■ ■

INTRODUCTION

What is it about horses that humans find so enthralling?

Trying to find the answer or indeed any answer to that age-old question was one of the reasons I became an equestrian journalist and author. Another reason was the delightful opportunity to meet and work with experienced and knowledgeable horse-people who, in the course of our labors, might provide insights into reasons for our affection for horses.

In the course of my career I compiled two collections of horse quotations. Many if not most of the quotes are in the volume you're holding in your hands or reading by means of an e-book. The quotations I selected provided special significance: a felicitous turn of phrase, an entertaining story, or a profound insight of the human-equine relationship. To coin a cliché, many quotations "took the words right out of my mouth," capturing thoughts and feelings that friends, colleagues, and I have tried to express not only to each other but to ourselves.

As Alexander Pope suggested, "True wit is nature to advantage dressed / What oft was said, but ne'er so well expressed." Perhaps you'll find that some "ne'er so well expressed" entries motivate you to further reading. If you discover an insight into riding or training or simply a new perspective about horses from anything here, imagine how much more you'll gain by exploring the full source in its original. Alas, too many of the books are out of print, but not all of them are, and a bit of time, effort, and ingenuity often pays off. If you draw a blank at bookstores, tack shops, or libraries, try book dealers and the internet.

You may well come across an old friend or two: a poem, short story, an excerpt from a novel, or another piece of literature you hadn't thought about in years. Those are friendships well worth renewing, and don't be surprised if you find yourself appreciating the work even more with the passage of time.

You may well be struck, as I was, by the range of people who had something to say about horses. Almost invariably, what they had to say was heartfelt or at least complimentary (Mark Twain being the most notable exception). It's an impressive array. Riders, trainers, and equestrian commentators stand alongside poets, novelists, and playwrights. "Anonymous" and "source unknown" are cheek by jowl next to well-known literary and equestrian figures.

What, then, is it about horses that has inspired so much emotion from so many generations of so many cultures?

Although quotations provide insights, there is no simple answer. The slices of prose and poetry that are in this book reflect diverse and often contradictory feelings of love, fear, awe, protectiveness, elation, frustration, companionship, and unalloyed joy. In short, the very same elements that forge relationships between humans and between humanity and the eternal.

And like the keys to these relationships, the secret of mankind's fascination with horses will forever remain a divine mystery locked in our hearts.

—Steven D. Price

Horses in Literature

I on my horse, and Love on me, doth try

Our horsemanships, while by strange work I prove

A horseman to my horse, a horse to Love,

And now man's wrongs in me, poor beast! decry.

The reins wherewith my rider doth me tie

Are humbled thoughts, which bit of reverence move,

Curb'd in with fear, but with gilt boss above

Of hope, which makes it seem fair to the eye:

The wand is will; thou, Fancy, saddle art,

Girt fast by Memory; and while I spur

My horse, he spurs with sharp desire my heart.

He sits me fast however I do stir,

And now hath made me to his hand so right,

That in the manage myself takes delight.

—SIR PHILIP SIDNEY, SONNET 49: "ON MY HORSE"

At one time the Horse had the plain entirely to himself. Then a Stag intruded into his domain and shared his pasture. The Horse, desiring to revenge himself on the stranger, asked a man if he were willing to help him in punishing the Stag. The man replied that if the Horse would receive a bit in his mouth and agree to carry him, he would contrive effective weapons against the Stag.

The Horse consented and allowed the man to mount him. From that hour he found that instead of obtaining revenge on the Stag, he had enslaved himself to the service of man.

—AESOP'S FABLES, "THE HORSE AND THE STAG"

When God created the horse He said to the magnificent creature:
I have made thee as no other. All the treasures of the earth lie
between thy eyes. Thou shalt carry my friends upon thy back.
Thy saddle shall be the seat of prayers to me. And thou fly
without wings, and conquer without any sword. Oh, horse.

—THE KORAN

Such horses are
The jewels of the horseman's hands and thighs,
They go by the word and hardly need the rein.
They bred such horses in Virginia then,
Horses that were remembered after death
And buried not so far from Christian ground
That if their sleeping riders should arise
They could not witch them from the earth again
And ride a printless course along the grass
With the old manage and light ease of hand.

—STEPHEN VINCENT BENÉT, *JOHN BROWN'S BODY*

But why discourse

Upon the Virtues of the Horse?

They are too numerous to tell

Save when you have a Horse to Sell.

—JOSH BILLINGS [HENRY WHEELER SHAW],
JOSH BILLINGS: HIS SAYINGS

A horse that can count to ten is a remarkable

horse, not a remarkable mathematician.

—SAMUEL JOHNSON, QUOTED IN *THE LIFE OF*
SAMUEL JOHNSON BY JAMES BOSWELL

They say princes learn no art truly, but the art of

horsemanship. The reason is, the brave beast is no flatterer.

He will throw a prince as soon as his groom.

—BEN JONSON, *EXPLORATA*

I give you horses for your games in May

And all of them well trained unto the course,

Each docile, swift, erect, a goodly horse;

With armour on their chests, and bells at play

Between their brows, and pennons fair and gay

Fine nets, and housings meet for warriors

Emblazoned with the shields ye claim for yours,

Gules, argent, or, all dizzy at noonday.

—ATTRIBUTED TO FOLGORE DI SAN GIMIGNANO

Four things greater than all things are—

Women and Horses and Power and War.

—RUDYARD KIPLING, "THE BALLAD OF THE KING'S JEST"

The horse, the horse! The symbol of surging potency

and power of movement, of action, in man.

—D. H. LAWRENCE, *APOCALYPSE*

A short life in the saddle, Lord!

Not long life by the fire.

—LOUISE IMOGEN GUINEY, "THE KNIGHT ERRANT"

A horse is a vain thing for safety.

—PSALMS 33:17

●

The revolution does not choose its paths: it made its first
steps toward victory under the belly of a Cossack's horse.

—LEON TROTSKY, *HISTORY OF THE RUSSIAN REVOLUTION*

●

Yet if man, of all the Creator plann'd
His noblest work is reckoned,
Of the works of His hand, by sea or land,
The horse may at least rank second.

—ADAM LINDSAY GORDON, "HIPPODROMANIA"

It takes a good deal of physical courage to ride a horse. This, however, I have. I get it at about forty cents a flask, and take it as required.

—STEPHEN LEACOCK, "REFLECTIONS ON RIDING," *LITERARY LAPSES*

Who drives the horses of the sun
Shall lord it but a day.

—JOHN VANCE CHENEY, "THE HAPPIEST HEART"

The same philosophy is a good horse in the stable, but an arrant jade on a journey.

—OLIVER GOLDSMITH, *THE GOOD NATUR'D MAN*

Be not elated at any excellence that is not your own. If the horse in his elation were to say, "I am beautiful," it could be endured; but when you say in your elation, "I have a beautiful horse," rest assured that you are elated at something good that belongs to a horse.

—EPICTETUS, *DISCOURSES*

"You know, Doctor," said the horse, "that vet over the hill knows nothing at all. He has been treating me six weeks now—for spavins. What I need is SPECTACLES. I am going blind in one eye. There's no reason why horses shouldn't wear glasses, the same as people."

—HUGH LOFTING, *DOCTOR DOLITTLE*

The horses, mares, and frisking fillies,

Clad, all, in linen white as lilies.

—ROBERT HERRICK, "THE HOCK-CART, OR HARVEST HOME"

Horses and men are just alike.

There was my stallion, Billy Lee,

Black as a cat and trim as a deer,

With an eye of fire, keen to start,

And he could hit the fastest speed

Of any racer around Spoon River.

—EDGAR LEE MASTERS, *SPOON RIVER ANTHOLOGY*

We should not even ignore those speculators on Reality
who doubted whether a white horse was real because
he was white, or because he was solid.

—KAKUZO OKAKURA, *THE BOOK OF TEA*

The love of horses which they had, alive,
And care of chariots, after death survive.

—VIRGIL, *THE AENEID*

O the horseman's and horsewoman's joys!
The saddle, the gallop, the pressure upon the seat,
the cool gurgling by the ears and hair.

—WALT WHITMAN, *LEAVES OF GRASS*

Somewhere . . . Somewhere in time's Own Space

There must be some sweet pastured place

Where creeks sing on and tall trees grow

Some Paradise where horses go,

For by the love that guides my pen

I know great horses live again.

—STANLEY HARRISON

Dear to me is my bonnie white steed;

Oft has he helped me at pinch of need.

—SIR WALTER SCOTT, "ROKEBY"

It makes men imperious to sit a horse.

—OLIVER WENDELL HOLMES SR., *THE AUTOCRAT OF THE BREAKFAST-TABLE*

Steeds, steeds, what steeds! Has the whirlwind a home in your manes?

—NIKOLAI GOGOL, *TARAS BULBA*

Let the best horse leap the hedge first.

—THOMAS FULLER, MD, *GNOMOLOGIA*

●

There is no need of spurs when a horse is running away.

—PUBLILIUS SYRUS, *MORAL SAYINGS*

●

Go anywhere in England, where there are natural, wholesome, contented and really nice English people, and what do you always find? That the stables are the real centre of the household.

—GEORGE BERNARD SHAW, *HEARTBREAK HOUSE*

A good horse should be seldom spurred.

—THOMAS FULLER, MD, *GNOMOLOGIA*

A lovely horse is always an experience . . . It is an emotional experience of the kind that is spoiled by words.

—BERYL MARKHAM, *WEST WITH THE NIGHT*

My horses understand me tolerably well; I converse with them at least four hours every day. They are strangers to bridle or saddle; they live in great amity with me, and friendship of each other.

—JONATHAN SWIFT, *GULLIVER'S TRAVELS*

Lived in his saddle, loved the chase, the course,

And always, ere he mounted, kiss'd his horse.

—WILLIAM COWPER, "CONVERSATIONS"

•

While his rider every hand survey'd,

Sprung loose, and flew into an escapade;

Not moving forward, yet with every bound

Pressing, and seeming still to quit his ground.

—JOHN DRYDEN, "ABSALOM AND ACHITOPHEL"

What a creature he was! Never have I felt such a horse between my knees. His great haunches gathered under him with every stride, and he shot forward ever faster and faster, stretched like a greyhound, while the wind beat in my face and whistled past my ears.

—SIR ARTHUR CONAN DOYLE, *THE ADVENTURES OF BRIGADIER GERARD*

With flowing tail and flying mane,
Wide nostrils, never stretched by pain,
Mouth bloodless to bit or rein,
And feet that iron never shod,
And flanks unscar'd by spur or rod.
A thousand horses—the wild—the free—
Like waves that follow o'er the sea,
Came thickly thundering on.

—GEORGE GORDON NOEL, LORD BYRON, *CHILDE HAROLD'S PILGRIMAGE*

He did not feel the ground under his feet . . . he thrust himself into the capriole, rose high in the air . . . forelegs and hindlegs horizontal. He soared above the ground, his head high in jubilation. Conquering!

—FELIX SALTEN, *FLORIAN*

I heard a neigh, Oh, such a brisk and melodious neigh it was. My very heart leaped with the sound.

—NATHANIEL HAWTHORNE, "THE CHIMAERA," *A WONDER BOOK FOR GIRLS AND BOYS*

On horseback he seemed to require as many hands as a
Hindu god, at least four for clutching the reins, and two
more for patting the horse soothingly on the neck.

—H. H. MUNRO [SAKI]

Take most people, they're crazy about cars. I'd rather have a
goddam horse. A horse is at least human, for godsake.

—J. D. SALINGER, *THE CATCHER IN THE RYE*

I love the horse from hoof to head.
From head to hoof and tail to mane.
I love the horse as I have said—
From head to hoof and back again.

—JAMES WHITCOMB RILEY, "I LOVE THE HORSE"

A fly, sir, may sting a stately horse, and make him wince;

but one is still an insect, and the other a horse still.

—SAMUEL JOHNSON, "ON CRITICS," QUOTED IN
THE LIFE OF SAMUEL JOHNSON BY JAMES BOSWELL

I am sick as a horse.

—LAURENCE STERNE, *TRISTRAM SHANDY*

The Horse's Prayer—

I'm only a horse, dear Master, but my heart is warm and true,

And I'm ready to work my hardest, for the pleasure of pleasing you.

Good corn, and hay, and water, are all that I wish to ask.

And a warm dry bed to rest on, when I've finished my daily task.

Don't strike me in needless anger if I'm slow to understand,

But encourage my drooping spirits with a gentle voice and hand.

Finally, O my master! When my health and strength are gone,

When I'm getting old and feeble, and my long life's work is done,

Don't sell me to cruel owners, to be slaved to my latest breath,

But grant me the untold blessing of a quick and painless death;

That, as you have always found me a patient and loyal friend,

The years of my faithful service may be crowned by a peaceful end.

I plead in the name of the Savior, Who cares when the sparrows fall.

Who was born in a lowly stable, and knows, and loves us all!

—ANONYMOUS, "THE HORSE'S PRAYER"

I pray that gentle hands may guide my feet;

I ask for kind commands from voices sweet;

At night a stable warm with scented hay,

Where, safe from every harm, I'll sleep till day.

—ANONYMOUS, "A PONY'S PRAYER"

Hobson's choice.

Tobias Hobson (died 1630) was the first man in England that let
out hackney horses. When a man came for a horse he was led
into the stable, where there was a great choice, but he obliged
him to take the horse which stood next to the stable-door; so that
every customer was alike well served according to his chance,—
from whence it became a proverb when what ought to be your
election was forced upon you, to say, "Hobson's choice."

**—ADDISON AND STEELE, *THE SPECTATOR*, NO. 509, QUOTED
IN *BARTLETT'S FAMILIAR QUOTATIONS* (1903 EDITION)**

A dog starv'd at his Master's Gate

Predicts the ruin of the State

A Horse misus'd upon the Road

Calls to Heaven for Human blood.

—WILLIAM BLAKE, "AUGURIES OF INNOCENCE"

●

I wheeled about,

Proud and exulting like an untired horse

That cares not for his home.

—WILLIAM WORDSWORTH, "INFLUENCE OF NATURAL
OBJECTS IN CALLING FORTH AND STRENGTHENING THE
IMAGINATION IN BOYHOOD AND EARLY YOUTH"

Strong is the horse upon his speed;

Strong in pursuit the rapid glede,

Which makes at once his game . . .

—CHRISTOPHER SMART, "A SONG TO DAVID"

Some men to carriages aspire;

On some the costly hansoms wait;

Some seek a fly, on job or hire;

Some mount the trotting steed, elate.

—AMY LEVY, "BALLADE OF AN OMNIBUS"

What transport in her bosom grew,

When first the horse appear'd in view!

—JOHN GAY, "THE HARE AND MANY FRIENDS"

●

The pamper'd horse is seldom seen in breath,

Whose manger makes his grace (oftimes) to melt . . .

—GEORGE GASCOIGNE, "FIE, PLEASURE, FIE!"

●

My little horse must think it queer

To stop without a farmhouse near

Between the woods and frozen lake

The darkest evening of the year.

—ROBERT FROST, "STOPPING BY WOODS
ON A SNOWY EVENING"

Boot, saddle, to horse and away!

Rescue my castle before the hot day

Brightens to blue from its silvery gray,

(Chorus) *Boot, saddle, to horse, and away!*

—ROBERT BROWNING, "CAVALIER TUNES: BOOT AND SADDLE"

Nothing made the horse so fat as the king's eye.

—PLUTARCH, *LIFE OF CICERO*

To hear the horse neigh to the drum and trumpet,

and the trumpet and war shout reply.

—WILLIAM BLAKE, "THE FRENCH REVOLUTION"

And there lay the steed with his nostril all wide,

But through it there rolled not the breath of his pride;

And the foam of his gasping lay white on the turf,

And cold as the spray of the rock-beating surf.

—GEORGE GORDON NOEL, LORD BYRON, "THE
DESTRUCTION OF SENNACHERIB"

Fall, Hercules, from heaven, in tempests hurl'd,

And cleanse this beastly stable of the world . . .

—GEORGE CHAPMAN, "THE SHADOW OF NIGHT"

And neigh like Boanerges;

Then, punctual as a star,

Stop—docile and omnipotent—

At its own stable door.

—EMILY DICKINSON, "THE RAILWAY TRAIN"

Mother dear, we cannot stay!

The wild white horses foam and fret.

—MATTHEW ARNOLD, "THE FORSAKEN MERMAN"

As Bayard feels his oats, and in his pride

Begins to skip and sidle from his course

Until he feels the whiplash, then he thinks,

"Although I prance first in the tandom traces

Plumb and well groomed, still I am just a horse

I must put up with horses' law and pull

With other fellow creatures . . .

—GEOFFREY CHAUCER, *TROILUS AND CRESSIDA*

Since then 'tis centuries; but each

Feels shorter than the day

I first surmised the horses' heads

Were toward eternity.

—EMILY DICKINSON, "THE CHARIOT (BECAUSE
I COULD NOT STOP FOR DEATH)"

To-night the very horses springing by

Toss gold from whitened nostrils.

—ARCHIBALD LAMPMAN, "WINTER EVENING"

One may lead a horse to water,

Twenty cannot make him drink.

—CHRISTINA ROSSETTI, "GOBLIN MARKET"

And that my Muse, to some ears not unsweet,

Tempers her words to trampling horses' feet

More oft than to a chamber melody.

—SIR PHILIP SIDNEY, *ASTROPHEL AND STELLA*, SONNET 84

But they must go, the time draws on,

And those white-favour'd horses wait;

They rise, but linger; it is late;

Farewell, we kiss, and they are gone.

—ALFRED, LORD TENNYSON, *IN MEMORIAM*,
"O! LIVING WILL THAT SHALT ENDURE"

O virgin, know'st thou not our steeds drink of the golden springs

Where Luvah doth renew his horses?

—WILLIAM BLAKE, *THE BOOK OF THEL*

And steeds, unbridled, sporting carelessly,

Crop the rank grass that on thy bosom grows . . .

—JOSEPH HOWE, "SABLE ISLAND"

As freely we rode on together

With helms unlaced and bridles slack.

—WILLIAM MORRIS, "RIDING TOGETHER"

Weel mounted on his grey mare, Meg,—

A better never lifted leg,—

Tam skelpit on thro' dub and mire,

Despising wind and rain and fire . . .

—ROBERT BURNS, "TAM O'SHANTER: A TALE"

His neck is high and erect, his head full with intelligence, his belly

short, his back full, and his proud chest swell with hard muscle.

—VIRGIL, *GEORGICS*

A horse thou knowest, a man thou dost not know.

—ALFRED, LORD TENNYSON, *IDYLLS OF*
THE KING, "GARETH AND LYNETTE"

Mares, she said, had not been altered, in them the blood
flowed freely, their life cycles had not been tampered
with, their natures were completely their own. The mare
usually had more energy than the gelding, could be as
temperamental as the stallion and was, in fact, its superior.

—JOHN HAWKES, *WHISTLEJACKET*

And the hoofs of the horses as they run shake the crumbling field.

—VIRGIL, *THE AENEID*

Whose only fit companion is his horse.

—WILLIAM COWPER, "CONVERSATION"

When I looked at life from the saddle and was as
near to heaven as it was possible to be.

—FRANCES, COUNTESS OF WARWICK, *DISCRETIONS*

Be it said in letters both bold and bright:

"Here is the steed that saved the day

By carrying Sheridan into the fight."

—THOMAS B. READ, "SHERIDAN'S RIDE"

Whose laughs are hearty, tho' his jests are coarse,

And loves you best of all things—but his horse.

—ALEXANDER POPE, "EPISTLE TO MRS.
THERESA BLOUNT ON HER LEAVING TOWN"

Every single movement of Florian's revealed nobility,
grace, significance and distinction all in one; and in each
of his poses he was the ideal model for a sculptor, the
composite of all the equestrian statues in history.

—FELIX SALTEN, *FLORIAN*

The mare . . . then set off for home with the speed of a swallow,
and going as smoothly and silently. I never had dreamed of such
delicate motion, fluent, and graceful, and ambient, soft as the
breeze flitting over the flowers but swift as the summer lightning.

—R. D. BLACKMORE, *LORNA DOONE*

Their [the Tartars'] horses are so well broken-in to quick changes of movement, that upon the signal given, they instantly turn in every direction; and by these rapid manoeuvers many victories have been won.

—MARCO POLO, *THE DIVERSITIES AND MARVELS OF THE WORLD*

The horses of Achilles stood apart from their battle weeping, because they had learned that their charioteer had fallen in the dust by the hand of man-slaying Hector. When Zeus saw how they grieved, he took pity on them. "Poor creatures, why did I give you to King Peleus, a mortal destined to die—you who are immortal."

—HOMER, *THE ILIAD*

"The great art of riding, as I was saying, is to keep your balance
properly. Like this, you know—" He let go the bridle and
stretched out both his arms to show Alice what he meant, and
this time he fell flat on his back, right under the horse's feet.
"Plenty of practice!" he went on repeating, all the time
that Alice was getting him on his feet again.

—LEWIS CARROLL, *THROUGH THE LOOKING GLASS*

I thought, at setting off, about two dozen
Cantos would do; but at Apollo's pleading
If that my Pegasus should not be founder'd,
I think to canter gently through a hundred.

—GEORGE GORDON NOEL, LORD BYRON, *DON JUAN*, CANTO 12

Dosn't thou 'ear my 'erse's legs, as they canters away?

Proputty, proputty, proputty—that's what I 'ears 'em say.

Proputty, proputty, proputty—Sam, thou's an ass for thy pains:

Theer's moor sense i' one o' 'is legs, nor in all thy brains.

—ALFRED, LORD TENNYSON,

"NORTHERN FARMER: NEW STYLE"

"Bitzer," said Thomas Gradgrind. "Your definition of a horse."

"Quadruped. Graminivorous. Forty teeth, namely twenty-four grinders, four eye-teeth, and twelve incisive. Sheds coat in the spring; in marshy countries, sheds hoofs, too. Hoofs hard, but requiring to be shod with iron. Age known by marks in mouth."

"Now girl number twenty," said Mr. Gradgrind.

"You know what a horse is."

—CHARLES DICKENS, *HARD TIMES*

Imagination is a good horse to carry you over the ground—not a flying carpet to set you free from improbability.

—ROBERTSON DAVIES, *THE MANTICORE*

Their land is full of horses,

There is no limit to their chariots.

—ISAIAH 2:7

It [the separation of the Baron's horse's hindquarters from its
forequarters] would have been an irreparable loss, had not our
farrier to bring both parts together while hot. He sewed them up
with sprigs and young shoots of laurels that were at hand. The
wound healed; and what could not have happened to so glorious
a horse, the sprigs took root in his body, grew up and formed
a bower over me, so that afterwards I could upon many other
expeditions in the shade of my own and my horse's laurels.

—RUDOLPH RASPE, *THE TRAVELS OF BARON MUNCHAUSEN*

When a harvester grows weary of his work, it is said "He has the fatigue of the Horse." The first sheaf, called the "Cross of the Horse," is placed on a cross of boxwood in the barn, and the youngest horse on the farm must tread on it.

—SIR JAMES FRAZER, *THE GOLDEN BOUGH*

Thou shall be for Man a source of happiness and wealth; thy back shall be a seat of honor, and thy belly of riches; every grain of barley given thee shall purchase indulgence for the sinner. All the treasures of this earth lie between thine eyes. Thou shalt cast Mine enemies beneath thy hooves . . . This shall be the seat from whence prayers rise unto me.

—THE KORAN

Show me a man who has no pity on his horse, and I will show you one who is a cruel husband, if he is married, and a tyrannical parent, if he has children; a man that would be Nero if he had the power. He is a coward by nature and a fiend by practice.

—GEORGE ELIOT, *MIDDLEMARCH*

When I was a child, I used to jump bareback over fences four
to four and a half feet high. I don't remember being afraid.
I think my mother took custody of the fear for me, and my
job was only not to fall off and not to let on how often I was
jumping. When I came back to riding at forty-four, though,
every little two-foot fence looked to me like a Puissance wall.

—JANE SMILEY, "PUISSANCE," IN *HORSE
PEOPLE*, EDITED BY MICHAEL J. ROSEN

"What need I got for a horse I would need
a bear trap to catch?" Eck said.
"Didn't you just see me catch him?"
"I seen you," Eck said. "And I don't want nothing as
big as a horse if I got to wrastle with it every time it
finds me on the same side of the fence it's on."

—WILLIAM FAULKNER, *SPOTTED HORSES*

To battle rode George Washington

Upon my grandsire's courser,

And when the victory was won

The courser was no more, sir.

That faithful steed had borne our race

In saddle, chaise and pillion;

My father never saw his face,

But called him worth a million.

—J. W. DEFOREST, "JUDGE BOODLE"

[Ayla] was thinking about naming the horse. I've never named anyone before. She smiled to herself. Wouldn't they think I was strange naming a horse. Not any stranger than living with one.

—JEAN M. AUEL, *THE VALLEY OF HORSES*

No pity I ask, and no counsel I need,

But bring me, O, bring me, my gallant young steed,

With his high archèd neck, and his nostril spread wide,

His eye full of fire, and his step full of pride!

As I spring to his back, as I seize the strong rein,

The strength to my spirit returneth again!

—GRACE GREENWOOD, "THE HORSEBACK RIDE"

As I ride, as I ride,

Ne'er has spur my swift horse plied,

Yet his hide, streaked and pied,

As I ride, as I ride,

Shows where sweat has sprung and dried,

—Zebra-footed, ostrich-thighed—

How has vied stride with stride

As I ride, as I ride!

—ROBERT BROWNING, "THROUGH THE
METIDJA TO ABD-EL-KADR"

Right into the stars he reared aloft, his red eye rolling and raging,

He whirled and sunfished and lashed, and rocked

the earth with thunder and flame.

He squealed like a regular devil horse. I was

haggard and spent and aging—

Roped clean, but almost storming clear, his fury too fierce to tame.

—WILLIAM ROSE BENÉT, "THE HORSE THIEF"

When walkin' down a city street,

Two thousand miles from home,

The pavestone hurtin' of the feet

That never ought to roam,

A pony just reached to one side

And grabbed me by the clothes;

He smelled the sagebrush, durn his hide!

You bet a pony knows!

—ARTHUR CHAPMAN, "THE MEETING"

Now the heart of a horse has love

For the master and home it knew:

And the mind of a horse can prove

That memory dwells there, too.

—ELLA WHEELER WILCOX, "THE HORSE"

What are we, we your horses,

So loyal where we serve,

Fashioned of noble forces

All sensitive with nerve?

Torn, agonized, we wallow

On the blood-bemired sod;

And still the shiploads follow.

Have horses then no God?

—KATHARINE LEE BATES, "THE HORSES"
[THE POEM BEGINS WITH A HEADNOTE: "THUS FAR
80,000 HORSES HAVE BEEN SHIPPED FROM THE UNITED
STATES TO THE EUROPEAN BELLIGERENTS."]

Eager as fire though the last goal is won,

These wilding creatures gentled to the rein,

These little brothers of the wind and sun.

—ELEANOR BALDWIN, "POLO PONIES"

Wherever thrumming hoofbeats drum
As galloping riders go or come;
Wherever a saddle is still a throne
And dust of hoofs by wind is blown;
Wherever are horsemen, young or old,
The Pacing Mustangs's tale is told.

—ANONYMOUS, "THE WHITE MUSTANG"

For of this savage race unbent
The ocean is the element.
Of old escaped from Neptune's car, full sure
Still with the white foam flick'd are they,
And when the seas puff black from gray,
And ships part cables, loudly neigh
The stallions of the Camargue, all joyful in the roar.

—GEORGE MEREDITH, "THE MARES OF THE CAMARGUE"

Let the Sultan bring his famous horses,

Prancing with their diamond-studded reins;

They, my darling, shall not match thy fleetness

When they course with thee the desert-plains.

—BAYARD TAYLOR, "HASSAN TO HIS MARE"

First horse: We are the pets of men—

The pampered pets of men!

There is naught for us too gentle and good

In the graceful days of our babyhood.

They hang our portraits on their walls,

And paint and garnish and gild our stalls.

Second horse: We are the slaves of men—

The menial slaves of men! . . .

In the winds of Winter, or Summer sun,

The tread of our toil is never done . . .

They draft us into their bloody spites,

They spur us, bleeding, into their fights . . .

—WILLIAM "WILL" MCKENDREE CARLETON,

"DIALOGUE OF THE HORSES"

No honors wait him, medal, badge or star,

Though scarce could war a kindlier deed unfold;

He bears within his breast, more precious far

Beyond the gift of kings, a heart of gold.

—ANONYMOUS, "GOODBYE, OLD FRIEND"
[INSPIRED BY AN INCIDENT ON THE ROAD TO A BATTERY
POSITION IN SOUTHERN FLANDERS DURING WORLD WAR I]

With flowing tail and flying mane,

Wide nostrils never stretch'd by pain,

Mouths bloodless to the bit or rein,

And feet that iron never shod,

And flanks unscarr'd by spur or rod,

A thousand horse, the wild, the free,

Like waves that follow o'er the sea,

Came thickly thundering on . . .

They stop, they start, they snuff the air,

Gallop a moment here and there,

Approach, retire, wheel round and round . . .

—GEORGE GORDON NOEL, LORD BYRON, *MAZEPPA*

The roan horse is young and will learn: the roan horse buckles into

harness and feels the foam on the collar at the end of a haul: the

roan horse points four legs to the sky and rolls in the red clover . . .

—CARL SANDBURG, "POTATO BLOSSOM SONGS AND JIGS"

Behold! in glittering show,

A gorgeous car of state!

The white-plumed steeds, in cloth of gold,

Bow down beneath its weight;

And the noble war-horse, led

Caparison'd along,

Seems fiercely for his lord to ask,

As his red eye scans the throng.

— LYDIA HUNTLEY SIGOURNEY,
"THE RETURN OF NAPOLEON FROM ST. HELENA"

The stallion flashed by the stands, going faster with every magnificent stride. With a sudden spurt he bore down on Sun Raider. For a moment he hesitated as he came alongside . . . Into the lead, the Black swept, past the cheering thousands—a step, a length, two lengths ahead—then the mighty giant plunged under the wire.

—WALTER FARLEY, *THE BLACK STALLION*

The thing about horses, he realized—and he never realized it until they were rolling on top of him in the dust, or rubbing him off against the side of a barn, trying to break his leg—was that if the horses didn't get broken, tamed, they'd just get wilder. There was nothing as wild as a horse that had never been broken. It just got meaner each day.

—RICK BASS, "WILD HORSES," IN *THE WATCH: STORIES*

Horses are not tamed by whips or blows. The strength of ten men is not so strong as a single strike of the hoof; the experience of ten men is not enough, for this is the unexpected, the unpredictable.

—BERYL MARKHAM, "THE SPLENDID OUTCAST," IN *THE SPLENDID OUTCAST: BERYL MARKHAM'S AFRICAN STORIES*

People, then, are not friend to horses unless
their horses love them in return.

—PLATO, *LYSIS*

We attended stables, as we attended church, in our
best clothes, no doubt showing the degree of respect
due to horses, no less than to the deity.

—SIR OSBERT SITWELL, *THE SCARLET TREE*

Take care to sell your horse before he dies.

The art of life is passing losses on.

—ROBERT FROST, QUOTED IN

ROBERT FROST: A LIFE BY JAY PARINI

What the horses o' Kansas think today, the horses of America
will think tomorrow; and I tell you that when the horses of
America rise in their might, the day o' the Oppressor is ended.

—RUDYARD KIPLING, *THE DAY'S WORK*

There is nothing in which a horse's power is better
revealed than in a neat, clean stop.

—MICHEL DE MONTAIGNE, QUOTED IN *SOME
HORSES* BY THOMAS MCGUANE

With easy seat behold them ride—

These are the Truly qualified—

Models of Sporting Men;

Graceful and elegant, yet neat;

Egad, the very sight's a treat

I long to have again!

—SOURCE UNKNOWN, QUOTED IN
SPORTING PRINTS BY F. L. WILDER

●

All in green went my love riding

On a great horse of gold

Into the silver dawn.

—E. E. CUMMINGS, "ALL IN GREEN WENT MY LOVE RIDING"

CENTAUR: One of a race of persons who lived before the division of labor had been carried to such a pitch of differentiation, and who followed the primitive economic maxim, "every man his own horse."

—AMBROSE BIERCE, *THE DEVIL'S DICTIONARY*

And now ascends the nostril-stream
Of stalwart horses come to plough.

—RICHARD HENRY HORNE, "THE PLOUGH"

But, snorting still with rage and fear,
He flew upon his far career;
At times I almost thought, indeed,
He must have slackened in his speed;
But no—my bound and slender frame
Was nothing to his angry might,
And merely like a spur became.

—GEORGE GORDON NOEL, LORD BYRON, *MAZEPPA*

In India, Prince Siddhartha, who was to become the Buddha, took great pride in his magnificent stallion Kanthaka. When he left his home, he called for his noble animal and spoke to him as a friend. "Today I go forth to seek supreme beatitude; lend me your help, O Kanthaka! Companions in arms or in pleasure are not hard to find, and we never want for friends when we set out to acquire wealth, but companions and friends desert us when it is the path of holiness we would take. "Yet of this I am certain: he who helps another to do good or to do evil shares in that good or in that evil. Know then, O Kanthaka, that it is a virtuous impulse that moves me. Lend me your strength and your speed. The world's salvation and your own is at stake."

—BRADLEY SMITH, *THE HORSE IN THE WEST*

The tygers of wrath are wiser than the horses of instruction.

—WILLIAM BLAKE, *SONGS OF INNOCENCE*

A groom used to spend whole days in currycombing and rubbing down his Horse, but at the same time stole his oats and sold them for his own profit. "Alas!" said the Horse, "if you really wish me to be in good condition, you should groom me less, and feed me more."

—*AESOP'S FABLES*, "THE HORSE AND THE GROOM"

What do we, as a nation, care about books? How much do you think we spend altogether on our libraries, public or private, as compared what we spend on our horses?

—JOHN RUSKIN, *SESAME AND LILIES*

Pat: He was an Anglo-Irishman.

Meg: In the blessed name of God, what's that?

Pat: A Protestant with a horse.

—BRENDAN BEHAN, *THE HOSTAGE*

Horse, thou art truly a creature without equal, for thou
fliest without wings and conquerest without a sword.

—THE KORAN

Whenever the moon and stars are set,

Whenever the wind is high,

All night long in the dark and wet,

A man goes riding by.

Late in the night when the fires are out,

Why does he gallop and gallop about?

—ROBERT LOUIS STEVENSON, "WINDY NIGHTS,"
IN *A CHILD'S GARDEN OF VERSES*

From the desert I come to thee

On a stallion shod with fire,

And the winds are left behind

In the speed of my desire.

—BAYARD TAYLOR, "BEDOUIN SONG"

A hurry of hooves in a village street,

A shape in the moonlight, a bulk in the dark,

And beneath, from the pebbles, in passing, a spark

Struck out by a steed flying fearless and fleet.

—HENRY WADSWORTH LONGFELLOW,
"THE MIDNIGHT RIDE OF PAUL REVERE"

Oh wasn't it naughty of Smudges?

Oh, Mummy, I'm sick with disgust.

She threw me in front of the Judges,

And my silly old collarbone's bust.

—SIR JOHN BETJEMAN, "HUNTER TRIALS"

●

He wheels his horse with a touch,

sword in hand.

How exquisite.

—A HAIKU BY YOSHIMOTO

Her hooves fly faster than ever flies the whirlwind,

Her tail-bone borne aloft, yet the hairs sweep the ground.

—ANONYMOUS ARABIAN POET, "THE IDEAL HORSE"

Stood up in the stirrups, leaned, patted his ear,

Called my Roland his pet-names, my horse without peer—

Clapped my hands, laughed and sang, any noise, bad or good,

Till at length into Aix Roland galloped and stood.

**—ROBERT BROWNING, "HOW THEY BROUGHT
THE GOOD NEWS FROM GHENT TO AIX"**

[And this parody:]

I unsaddled the saddle, unbuckled the bit,

Unshackled the bridle (the bit didn't fit)

And ungalloped, ungalloped, ungalloped, ungalloped a bit.

**—R. J. YEATMAN AND W. C. SELLAR, "HOW I BROUGHT
THE GOOD NEWS FROM AIX TO GHENT (OR VICE VERSA)"**

Horse People may be heads of state or professionally unemployed in their private lives, but horses are their passion, as Jerusalem was the passion of a soldier in some ancient crusade. The cult of the horse as their idol is as central to their lives as cocaine is to some and applause is to others.

—JUDITH KRANTZ, *PRINCESS DAISY*

Spur not an unbroken horse.

—SIR WALTER SCOTT, *THE MONASTERY*

I saw him out riding in the Row, clutching

to his horse like a string of onions.

—MARGOT ASQUITH, *THE AUTOBIOGRAPHY OF MARGOT ASQUITH*

Horse: A neighing quadruped, used in war, and draught and carriage.

—SAMUEL JOHNSON, *DICTIONARY OF THE ENGLISH LANGUAGE*

The Scythian cavalry regiments indeed resound with famous stories

of horses: a chieftain was challenged to a duel by an enemy and

killed, and when his adversary came to strip his body of his armor,

his horse kicked him and bit him till he died; another horse, when

his blinkers were removed and it found out that the mare he had

covered was his dam, made for a precipice and committed suicide.

—PLINY THE ELDER, *NATURAL HISTORY*

The steed bit his master;

How came this to pass?

He heard the good pastor

Cry, "All flesh is grass."

—ANONYMOUS, "ON A CLERGYMAN'S HORSE BITING HIM"

⬤

They head the list

Of bad to bet on,

But I insist

They're worse to get on.

—RICHARD ARMOUR, "HORSES"

⬤

No gymnastics could be better or harder exercise, and this and the art of riding, are of all the arts the most befitting a free man . . .

—PLATO, *LACHES*

You can't control a young horse unless you can control yourself.

—LINCOLN STEFFENS, *THE AUTOBIOGRAPHY OF LINCOLN STEFFENS*

Must we drag on this stupid existence forever,

So idly and weary, so full of remorse,

While everyone else takes his pleasure, and never

Seems happy unless he is riding a horse?

—EDWARD LEAR, *LAUGHABLE LYRICS*

Some people object to high-blowers, that is, 'osses wot make
a noise like steam-engines as they go. I don't see no great
objection to them myself, and think the use they are of
clearin' the way in crowded thoroughfares, and the protection
they afford in dark night by preventin' people ridin' against
you, more than counterbalance any disconvenience.

—ROBERT SMITH SURTEES [JOHN JORROCK], *HANDLEY CROSS*

As a boy in a prairie town I early learned to revere the work horse. To me, as to all boys, a dog was a slave, but a horse was a hero. And the men who handled him were heroes too.

—JAMES STEVENS, *HORSES*

Now whether the tall horse, in the natural playfulness of his disposition, was desirous of having a little innocent recreation with Mr. Winkle, or whether it occurred to him that he could perform the journey as much to his own satisfaction without a rider as with one, are points upon which, of course, we can arrive at no distinct conclusion.

—CHARLES DICKENS, *THE PICKWICK PAPERS*

Then there was the bridle. Billy explained how to use a stick of licorice for a bit until Galiban was used to having something in his mouth. Billy explained, "Of course we could force-break him to everything, but he wouldn't be as good a horse if we did. He'd always be a bit afraid, and he wouldn't mind because he wanted to."

—JOHN STEINBECK, *THE RED PONY*

"Will you lend me your mare to go a mile?"
"No, she is lame leaping over a stile."
"But if you will her to me spare,
You should have money for your mare."
"Oh ho, say you so?
Money will make the mare go."

—OLD ENGLISH SONG

The Associated Press reports carrying the news of Mary White's death declared that it came as a result from the fall from a horse. How she would have hooted at that! She never fell from a horse in her life. Horses have fallen on her and with her—"I'm always trying to hold 'em in my lap," she used to say. But she was proud of few things, and one was that she could ride anything that had four legs and hair.

—WILLIAM ALLEN WHITE, "MARY WHITE"
[THE NEWSPAPER EDITOR'S OBITUARY FOR HIS DAUGHTER]

Remember, a horse can tell you a lot of things, if you watch, and expect it to be sensible and intelligent.

—MARY O'HARA, MY FRIEND FLICKA

A man in passion rides a mad horse.

—BENJAMIN FRANKLIN, *POOR RICHARD'S ALMANACK*

In Aberdeenshire the last sheaf [of wheat] or "Maiden" is carried home in merry procession by the harvesters. It is then presented to the mistress of the house, who dresses it up to be preserved until the first mare foals. The Maiden is then taken down and presented to the mare as its first food. The neglect of this would have untoward effects upon the foal.

—SIR JAMES FRAZER, *THE GOLDEN BOUGH*

Come off to the stable, all you who are able,

And give your horses some oats and some corn;

For if you don't do it, your colonel will know it,

And then you will rue it, as sure as you're born.

—WORDS TO THE "STABLE CALL" CAVALRY BUGLE CALL

Ay, they heard his foot upon the stirrup,

And the sound of iron on stone

And how the silence surged softly backward

When the plunging hoofs were gone.

—WALTER DE LA MARE, "THE LISTENERS"

Let me leap into the saddle once more.

—HERMAN MELVILLE, *WHITE JACKET*

Powerful loin, and quarter wide,

Grace and majesty allied,

Basic power—living force—

Equine king—the Clydesdale horse.

—ANONYMOUS, "THE CLYDESDALE HORSE"

He [Rumbold] never would believe that Providence had sent
a few men into the world ready booted and spurred to ride,
and millions ready saddled and bridled to be ridden.

—THOMAS BABINGTON MACAULAY, *HISTORY OF ENGLAND*

●

I had a little pony,
His name was Dapple Gray;
I lent him to a lady
To ride a mile away;
She whipped him, she slashed him,
She rode him through the mire;
I would not lend my pony now
For all the lady's hire.

—ANONYMOUS, "I HAD A LITTLE PONY"

So hurry to see your lady,

Like a stallion on the track.

—ANONYMOUS LOVE SONG OF THE NEW

KINGDOM OF ANCIENT EGYPT

Shoe the horse, shoe the mare,

But let the little horse go bare.

—ANONYMOUS, "SHOE THE HORSE"

He that makes an ass of himself must not take it ill if men ride him.

—THOMAS FULLER, MD, *GNOMOLOGIA*

●

And here I say to parents, and especially to wealthy parents, Don't give your son money. As far as you can afford it, give him horses. No one ever came to grief—except honourable grief—through riding horses. No hour of life is lost that is spent in the saddle. Young men have often been ruined through owning horses, or through backing horses, but never through riding them; unless of course they break their necks, which, taken at a gallop, is a very good death to die.

—SIR WINSTON CHURCHILL, *MY EARLY LIFE*

"Ain't you never heard what Peter done?

Run the quarter-mile in twenty-one

And he run it backwards in twenty flat;

Why, stranger, where have you been at?"

"What else could he do,

This Peter McCue?"

"He could gallop the range with tireless legs,

He could build a fire and scramble the eggs;

Though he never learned to subtract or divide,

He was mighty good when he multiplied."

—ANONYMOUS, "PETER MCCUE" [CELEBRATING THE
VERSATILITY OF A NINETEENTH-CENTURY QUARTER HORSE]

Love animals. God has given them the rudiments of thought and joy untroubled. Do not trouble their joy, do not harass them, do not deprive them of their happiness, do not work against God's intention.

—FYODOR DOSTOYEVSKY, *THE BROTHERS KARAMAZOV*

For never man had friend

More enduring to the end,

Truer mate in every turn of time and tide.

Could I think we'd meet again

It would lighten half my pain?

At the place where the old horse died.

—G. J. WHYTE-MELVILLE, "THE PLACE
WHERE THE OLD HORSE DIED"

And he arched his neck, so graceful, and he tossed his tail, so saucy,

Like a proudly waving plume long and black!

He was light of hoof and fleet, I was supple, firm in seat,

And no sort of thing with feet, anywhere

In the country, could come nigh us; scarce the swallows could outfly us;

But the planet spun beneath us, and the sky went whizzing by us,

In the hurricane we made of the air.

—ROBERT W. SERVICE, "OLD ROBIN"

A bad-tempered man will never make a good-tempered horse.

—ANNA SEWELL, *BLACK BEAUTY*

Men are generally more careful of the breeding of
their horses and dogs than of their children.

—WILLIAM PENN, *SOME FRUITS OF SOLITUDE,
IN REFLECTIONS AND MAXIMS RELATING
TO THE CONDUCT OF HUMAN LIFE*

And I looked, and beheld a pale horse: and his name that
sat upon him was Death, and Hell followed with him.

—REVELATION 6:8

I love the disciplined panic of a horse flirting with a tantrum at every turn, the delicate voluptuous play of muscles, the grace-sprung power.

—DIANE ACKERMAN, "ASTRIDE THE TWILIGHT," IN *HORSE PEOPLE*, EDITED BY MICHAEL J. ROSEN

What delight to back the flying steed that challenges the wind for speed! . . . Whose soul is in his task, turns labour into sport!

—JAMES SHERIDAN KNOWLES, *THE LOVE CHASE*

The ego's relation to the id might be compared to that of the rider to his horse. The horse supplies the locomotive energy, while the rider has the privilege of deciding on the goal and of guiding the powerful animal's movement.

—SIGMUND FREUD, *NEW INTRODUCTORY LECTURES ON PSYCHO-ANALYSIS*

My beautiful! my beautiful!

That standeth meekly by

With thy proudly arch'd and glossy neck,

And dark and fiery eye;

The stranger hath they bridle-rein,

Thy master hath his gold;

Fleet limbed and beautiful, farewell;

Thou'rt sold; my steed, thou'rt sold.

—CAROLINE ELIZABETH SHERIDAN NORTON,
"THE ARAB'S FAREWELL TO HIS STEED"

Horses: the feeling of the absolute ancientness of the English
landscape. A landscape that should always, by rights, have horses in it.

So, too, should the landscape of the English mind.

—SIMON BARNES, "ENTHRALLED BY THE VIEW FROM
JASPER'S BACK," IN THE *TIMES* (LONDON), MAY 29, 1999

Content with harmless sport and simple food,

Boundless in faith and love and gratitude;

Happy the man, if there be any such—

Of whom his epitaph can say as much.

—ROBERT LOWE, LORD SHERBROOKE, "A HORSE'S EPITAPH"

Where in this world can man find nobility without pride,

friendship without envy, beauty without vanity? Here, where

grace is laced with muscle, and strength by gentleness confined.

He serves without servility; he has fought without enmity. There

is nothing so powerful, nothing less violent; there is nothing

so quick, nothing more patient. England's past has been borne

on his back. All our history is his industry: we are his heirs,

he is our inheritance. Ladies and gentlemen: The Horse!

**—ROBERT DUNCAN'S "TRIBUTE TO THE HORSE" [READ AT THE
CONCLUSION OF EVERY HORSE OF THE YEAR SHOW IN LONDON]**

■ ■ ■ ■ ■ ■ ■ ■ ■

Riding and Training

It's what you learn after you know it all that's important.

—LEGENDARY CALIFORNIA RIDER AND
TRAINER JIMMY WILLIAMS

●

Riding is simple . . . it's just not easy.

—ANONYMOUS

●

Know what you're going to have to do, and allow
yourself plenty of time to do it in.

—WILLIAM STEINKRAUS, *RIDING AND JUMPING*

Some people think horses are dumb. Ability and intelligence are
in all horses, regardless of breed. Their so-called stupidity stems
from our poor communication. Training a horse is like drawing a
picture. The better I draw the picture, the better the communication.
If I'm drawing a horse in pencil, I've communicated something.
If I add crayon to my drawing, you can then tell that the horse
I've drawn is a Palomino. Does that mean that you've gotten
smarter? No. It means that I've become a better communicator.

—JOHN LYONS, WITH SINCLAIR BROWN, *LYONS ON HORSES*

Intimate acquaintance with the horse's knowledge and leading
the kind of life that entails the continual reimaginings of
horsemanship mark the faces of some older riders with the look
that I have also seen on the faces of a few poets and thinkers, the
incandescent gaze of unmediated awareness that one might be
tempted to call innocence, since it is not unlike the gaze on the
face of a child absorbed in Tinkertoys or a beautiful bug, but it is
an achieved or restored innocence, and it is also terrible, the way
Pasternak's face was terrible in its continuing steadiness of gaze.

—VICKI HEARNE, *ADAM'S TASK*

We quickly learned that Max [Uncle Max, Shapiro's show jumper] possessed several serious quirks which we would need to iron out. My number one problem was mounting. As soon as Max knew I was aiming for the saddle, he would be off and running. We decided that the element of surprise would be our only hope. It was not uncommon to see me leaping onto the saddle from the hood of a car, a bale of hay or even a rooftop.

—OLYMPIC SHOW-JUMPING RIDER NEAL SHAPIRO, "FROM UNCLE MAX TO A MEDAL," IN *THE U.S. EQUESTRIAN TEAM BOOK OF RIDING*, EDITED BY WILLIAM STEINKRAUS

●

When riding a high-strung horse, pretend you are riding an old one.

—DOMINIQUE BARBIER, *SOUVENIR*

Teaching a horse to jump fences is more like instructing a
child to read than like training a dog to stay or fetch.
—HOLLY MENINO, *FORWARD MOTION*

●

What does it take to train a horse? More time than the horse has.
—FORMER ALL-AROUND RODEO CHAMPION LARRY MAHAN

●

Anything forced and misunderstood can never be beautiful.
And to quote the words of Simon: If a dancer was forced to
dance by whip and spikes, he would be no more beautiful
than a horse trained under similar conditions.
—XENOPHON, 400 BC

Every time you ride, you're either teaching or un-teaching your horse.

—GORDON WRIGHT

What is it that makes horses give their rider everything? It can only be a reaction based on mutual trust. Once a horse trusts his partner, he develops and grows; and once a rider has found trust in his horse's abilities, he can develop the confidence needed to achieve special accomplishments.

—ELIZABETH FURTH, *VISIONS OF SHOW JUMPING*

Riding is a partnership. The horse lends you his strength, speed and grace, which are greater than yours. For your part you give him your guidance, intelligence and understanding, which are greater than his. Together you can achieve a richness that alone neither can.

—LUCY REES, *THE HORSE'S MIND*

To make a perfect horseman, three things are requisite. First, to know how and when to help your horse. Secondly, how and when to correct him. And thirdly, how and when to praise him and to make much of him.

—THOMAS BLUNDEVILLE

Half the failures in life arise from pulling in one's horse as he is leaping.

—JULIUS AND AUGUSTUS HARE, *GUESSES AT TRUTH*

The horse you get off is not the same as the horse
you got on; it is your job as a rider to ensure that as
often as possible the change is for the better.

—ANONYMOUS

A good trainer can hear a horse speak to him.
A great trainer can hear him whisper.

—MONTY ROBERTS, *THE MAN WHO LISTENS TO HORSES*

I don't help people with horse problems, I
help horses with people problems.
—NICHOLAS EVANS, *THE HORSE WHISPERER*

●

A horseman should know neither fear, nor anger.
—ATTRIBUTED TO JAMES RAREY

●

An extra pressure, a silent rebuke, an unseen praising, a firm
correction: all these passed between us as through telegraph wires.
—CHRISTILOT HANSON-BOYLEN

The one best precept—the golden rule in dealing with
a horse—is never to approach him angrily. Anger is so
devoid of forethought that it will often drive a man to
do things which in a calmer mood he will regret.

—XENOPHON, *ON HORSEMANSHIP*

It's a lot like nuts and bolts—if the rider's nuts, the horse bolts!

—NICHOLAS EVANS, *THE HORSE WHISPERER*

It is the best of lessons if the horse gets a season of repose
whenever he has behaved to his rider's satisfaction.

—XENOPHON, *ON HORSEMANSHIP*

Whatever your purpose in riding, be sure that it includes the elements of fun and appreciation of your horse. Then you will be well on your way to becoming a true horseman.

—SHEILA WALL HUNDT, *INVITATION TO RIDING*

●

When the rider is thrown or is unable to make his mount do what he wants, it is always the horse that is blamed. When a horseman takes a spill, he looks to himself for the cause.

—MARGARET CABELL SELF, "HORSEMAN (VERSUS RIDER)," *THE HORSEMAN'S ENCYCLOPEDIA*

Women who have had the same opportunities as men of learning
to ride, ride quite as well as they. But as a rule they do not *get*
the chance of excelling, nor are they "set right" by unpalatable
home truths being told them without favour or affection.

—ALICE HAYES, *THE HORSEWOMAN*

To practice equestrian art is to establish a conversation on a
higher level with the horse; a dialogue of courtesy and finesse.

—NUNO OLIVEIRA, *REFLECTIONS ON EQUESTRIAN ART*

If the rider's heart is in the right place, his seat
will be independent of his hands.

—PIERO SANTINI, *THE FORWARD IMPULSE*

I've found that my most successful horses . . . all have certain traits in common. They're all very brave, good movers and solid individuals jumping, with the boldness to attack the cross-country courses. All of these horses in their own way are a bit difficult and are not to be ridden by a beginner. They're like John McEnroe of tennis: while they may be difficult, this strong character is what it takes to be an event horse.

—MIKE HUBER, "GETTING STARTED IN EVENTING,"
IN *RIDING FOR AMERICA*, EDITED BY NANCY JAFFER

Equestrian art, however, is something else which involves complete
harmony between horse and rider, and that makes the rider feel
that there have been moments of beauty and greatness which
make a flight possible from all that is ordinary and mediocre.

—NUNO OLIVEIRA, *NOTES AND REMINISCENCES
OF A PORTUGUESE RIDER*

You cannot train a horse with shouts and expect it to obey a whisper.

—DAGOBERT D. RUNES, *LETTERS TO MY SON*

Eventing has been called the ultimate equestrian challenge, and
not without reason. The event horse is the embodiment of courage,
speed, dexterity, power, scope, precision, durability and a resolute
will to prevail. The event rider, while possessing similar virtues
in plentiful measure, must be able to elicit from a horse, within
prudent limits, the willingness to deliver its talents on request, no
matter how challenging the obstacle or how taxing the pace.

—GARY J. BENSON, WITH PHIL MAGGITTI, *IN THE IRONS*

One of the most widely quoted of all riding axioms [is] Gustav Steinbrecht's "Ride your horse forward and hold it straight." Yet this trenchant advice of the great German horseman and writer is deceptive because it seems so simple, and so easy to put into practice; but those who have begun to really explore its richness of allusion will usually follow the quotation with "yes, that is the difficult thing." By the time the serious rider has learned why this is true, he will also know what riding in its best sense is all about.

—WILLIAM STEINKRAUS, *RIDING AND JUMPING*

For some people, working with the horse is just a way of stroking their own egos. Sometimes they have a lot of emotional baggage. Sometimes they lack awareness of their surroundings.

That's why horses have so many problems with humans.

—TRAINER BUCK BRANNAMAN [ONE OF THE INSPIRATIONS FOR *THE HORSE WHISPERER*], QUOTED IN *SMITHSONIAN MAGAZINE*

My first school horse was Pluto Kerka, who reminded me immediately and unmistakably that the reins were for the horse to be guided and not for the rider to hold on to. When my contact grew too strong, he leaned on the rein with all his weight or he rushed off. He could not have demonstrated more clearly how important it is to have an independent seat.

—ALOIS PODHAJSKY, *MY HORSES, MY TEACHERS*

Learning about our horses is learning about ourselves
as well, seeing how our personalities mesh or clash
with the horses we choose to ride or train.
—LINDA TELLINGTON-JONES, *GETTING IN TOUCH:*
UNDERSTAND AND INFLUENCE YOUR HORSE'S PERSONALITY

A rider's total belief in an instructor is, of course,
another essential. When students doubt me a little, I
suggest other teachers they should go to. Without belief,
discipline is a mockery, if not downright impossible.
—GEORGE H. MORRIS, *GEORGE H. MORRIS*
TEACHES BEGINNERS TO RIDE

Everyone who wants justly to call himself—or herself—a rider
should ponder the following statement very seriously: 99 per
cent of all horses have quite a number of bad habits which are
commonly put down to disobedience. And 99 per cent of all riders
do not understand how to break their horses of such habits.
—WILHELM MÜSELER, *RIDING LOGIC*

A real horseman must not only be an expert—he must also be
able to think and feel like a horse, that is, to realize that a horse
is not equipped with *human* understanding. Such a horseman
should be both horse and man—a centaur, not only physically,
but also psychologically—anthropomorphic and hippomorphic.

—WALDEMAR SEUNIG, *HORSEMANSHIP*

The noblest task of the riding teacher is to form
the mind of the student as well, so that the latter
comes to depend on the teacher less and less.

—WALDEMAR SEUNIG, *HORSEMANSHIP*

The right way to do almost anything with horses is mainly a matter of using your natural intelligence in an uncomplicated manner, and this holds true also for the rider's basic mounted position. Simplicity and economy of movement are the goals of classical technique; the position of the rider upon the horse is the first fundamental.

—GEORGE H. MORRIS, *HUNTER SEAT EQUITATION*

The quality of the jump is determined by the quality of the approach to the fence, which is itself determined by the quality of the getaway from the previous fence and the turns between the two jumps.

—MARY WANLESS, *THE NATURAL RIDER*

When your horse has reached his potential, leave it. It's such
a nice feeling when you and your horses are still friends.

—DR. REINER KLIMKE, OLYMPIC DRESSAGE GOLD MEDALIST
FOR GERMANY, QUOTED IN *HORSEPLAY* MAGAZINE

The most important principle is to want to do it, to be committed
before you start off to getting to the other side of every fence
every time . . . If you are not certain about whether you want
to go or not, do yourself and your horse a favor—don't start.

—CAPT. MARK PHILLIPS, *THE HORSE
AND HOUND BOOK OF EVENTING*

I have often thought that "pride goeth before a fall" must have
been written expressly for those riders who are too proud to reach
for the mane, or to get their hands up before a jump, but not too
proud to come back on their horse's mouth in mid-air, ruin a horse's
mouth and disposition, and finally, run the risk of falling off.

—GORDON WRIGHT, *LEARNING TO RIDE, HUNT, AND SHOW*

If I had to pick one thing that I had to hang my hat on, I would want the horse I was going to buy to have a face that I would enjoy seeing poked over the stall webbing every morning, waiting for breakfast.

—JAMES C. WOFFORD, *TRAINING THE THREE-DAY EVENT HORSE AND RIDER*

Perfect harmony between the rider and his horse, i.e., beauty, is the ultimate goal of all dressage. The horse must be visibly at ease, and nothing in the rider's demeanor should betray how hard the road is.

—WILHELM MÜSELER, *RIDING LOGIC*

Nanticoke [a show jumper of the 1960s] reinforced a lesson I'd already started to learn from other horses: never try to muscle your way with a horse. There may or may not be an ideal way to do things; but in the horse world you have to be realistic, willing to try different solutions to a problem until you find one that works both for you and the horse. Letting Nanticoke jog along while I mounted wasn't ideal, but it was good horsemanship because we started the ride relaxed instead of with a fight.

—GRAND PRIX RIDER AND TRAINER RODNEY JENKINS, IN *PRACTICAL HORSEMAN'S BOOK OF RIDING, TRAINING & SHOWING HUNTERS & JUMPERS*, EDITED BY M. A. STONERIDGE

As far as I'm concerned, a rider's fear is *real*—it's a non-negotiable issue. What feels like to her is what it is. Period. It doesn't matter whether her trainer, buddy, college professor, mother, or grandfather thinks she is overreacting, overprotective, or overindulgent.

—JANET SASSON EDGETTE, PSYD, *HEADS UP! PRACTICAL SPORTS PSYCHOLOGY FOR RIDERS, THEIR FAMILIES AND THEIR TRAINERS*

Man has always attempted to become one with his horse when in the saddle, and he constantly seeks moments of perfect mutuality of movement, moments in which the skill becomes an art—if only for the duration of a heartbeat.

—HANS-HEINRICH ISENBART, *THE BEAUTY OF THE HORSE*

Talk to a dreamer and get caught up in the excitement.
Sit on a fabulous horse and dream about having a horse
of such quality to ride. Go to the big shows. Watch the
great riders and dare to think . . . That could be me.

—JANE SAVOIE, *THAT WINNING FEELING! A NEW
APPROACH TO RIDING USING PSYCHOCYBERNETICS*

●

The rider, being the senior partner, has to make all efforts to learn the
language of the horse, and to speak to him by means of that dialect.

—LT. COL. A. L. D'ENDRÖDY, *GIVE YOUR HORSE A CHANCE*

Prejudice is ugly in any form. There is not one breed of horse
that is better than all others, or one best breed. Each has been
bred for specific characteristics. A Paso Fino is not bred to pull
a heavy wagon, few draft horses compete in calf roping, and a
Quarter Horse is not designed to run a hundred-mile race. But
there are more differences within a breed, than between breeds.

—JOHN LYONS, WITH SINCLAIR BROWN, *LYONS ON HORSES*

Show jumping . . . forms a partnership consisting of two performers
who metamorphose into one: knowledge and intuition on behalf
of the rider, together with a willingness on behalf of the horse. A
willingness that has emerged out of a mutual understanding and trust.

—ELIZABETH FURTH, *VISIONS OF SHOW JUMPING*

Riding allows me to distance myself from life's daily occurrences. When I am on a horse I forget everything else. I am absorbed by what I do. It is a certain escapism. When sitting on a horse my mind reaches a higher plane, especially when walking on a loose rein!

—JEAN-LOUIS GUNTZ, QUOTED IN *VISIONS OF DRESSAGE* BY ELIZABETH FURTH

There is a secret pleasing and cherishing of the horse with the bridle, which the rider must accomplish with so unperceiving a motion that none but the beast may know it.

—GERVASE MARKHAM, *THE COMPLEAT HORSEMAN*

There are a million miles of difference between the words "win" and "beat." We don't even allow the word "beat" on this farm. Because when you start talking about beating someone, you've lost your concentration. You're thinking about the opposition.

—SADDLE-SEAT TRAINER HELEN CRABTREE,
IN *CLASSIC* MAGAZINE

When in doubt, ride with your instincts.

—PAMELA C. BIDDLE AND JOEL E. FISHMAN,
ALL I NEED TO KNOW I LEARNED FROM MY HORSE

The worst fault a horse can exhibit in competition
is the lack of honesty, for just as this is a major
character flaw in a human, so it is in a horse.

—ANNA JANE WHITE-MULLINS,
JUDGING HUNTERS AND HUNTER SEAT EQUITATION

The secrets of successful training are to work out what you
want the horse to do and to explain to him in a way that he
can understand; as a successful trainer of novice show jumpers
once said, "training is just a series of repeated aids."

— CAROLYN HENDERSON AND LYNN RUSSELL,
BREAKING AND SCHOOLING

You could put wings on some horses and not get
them over [fences], they need to have heart.

— SHOW-JUMPING SUPERSTAR RIDER RODNEY JENKINS,
QUOTED IN *CLEAR ROUND* BY JULIA LONGLAND

For me, it is no good doing a lot of talking, or asking endless advice.
I have to school myself to tackle it alone because when it comes to
it, in the ring, you and the horse are out there on your own, and *you*
have to make the decisions, be wrapped up in what you're doing.

— BRITISH SHOW-JUMPING RIDER GRAHAM FLETCHER,
QUOTED IN *CLEAR ROUND* BY JULIA LONGLAND

Two words not commonly related to winning or losing at the horse show ring correlate to the color of the ribbons received. The two words are "act" and "react." Winners act. Nonwinners react.

—DON BURT, *WINNING WITH THE AMERICAN QUARTER HORSE*

But whether you regard the horse with awe or love, it is impossible to escape the sheer power of his presence, the phenomenal influence he exerts on the lives of all of us who decided at some stage that we wanted to become riders.

—MARY WANLESS, *THE NATURAL RIDER*

It is the very difficult horses that have the most to give you.

—LENDON GRAY

Horses are as much athletes as gymnasts, ballet dancers,
or ice skaters, and unless they learn how to understand
and use their bodies by "basic training," they can't be
expected to perform well when the going gets tough.
—JOY SLATER, WITH STEVEN D. PRICE, *RIDING'S A JOY*

No time spent in the saddle is wasted; as you learn to
communicate with the horse and appreciate what he can do
for you, it will add a fascinating dimension to your life.
—MARY GORDON-WATSON, *THE HANDBOOK OF RIDING*

The left side is the right side, and the right side is the wrong side.
—MAXIM ABOUT WHERE TO MOUNT AND DISMOUNT

All King Edward's Horses Canter Many Big Fences.

—MNEMONIC FOR THE A-K-E-H-C-M-B-F
LETTERS AROUND A DRESSAGE ARENA

Furthermore, in a successful partnership, the rider has to
know when he has to back off. He has to realize to what
degree he can tolerate a horse's idiosyncrasies. He has to
have a feeling for when he should enforce his own style
onto the horse and when he has to accept the horse's.

—ELIZABETH FURTH, *VISIONS OF SHOW JUMPING*

Ride your horse as you feel him, provided you were born to,
or over the years have learned to feel! It is the one thing
no book can teach you, no teacher can give you, the one
conquest of the laurels which will be entirely yours.

—JEAN FROISSARD, *CLASSICAL HORSEMANSHIP FOR OUR TIME*

A horseman is one who not only rides (although some fine horsemen do not ride at all) but also seeks to *know* the horse—its nature, needs and management—and feels a deep responsibility for his horses, the care they get, and the life they lead.

—SUSAN HARRIS, IN *THE AMERICAN JUMPING STYLE* BY GEORGE H. MORRIS

Natural talent, no matter how great, can't make up for a lack of basic knowledge and skills—but solid basics, combined with real desire and commitment, can make any rider a good rider.

—ANNE KURSINSKI, WITH MIRANDA LORRAINE,
ANNE KURSINSKI'S RIDING AND JUMPING CLINIC

Horses will always be stronger than humans, but luckily we have a slight edge in the brains department, and through centuries of trial and error we have developed a number of effective ways of getting horses to do what we want.

—BARBARA BURN, THE HORSELESS RIDER

A rider has to be able to judge whether a horse is physically and mentally strong enough to carry out what has been asked for. In this way a horse will never get into a stressful situation. It is so important to ask oneself: "If the horse could talk and I was to ask it whether it actually knows what I want from it, would it reply, 'No idea!' or 'Yes, of course I do. I'm just not quite strong enough yet.'"

—ARTHUR KOTTAS-HELDENBERG, QUOTED IN
VISIONS OF DRESSAGE BY ELIZABETH FURTH

Fear almost always arises—in horses as well as in people—from concern about what might happen, and much more rarely from what *is* happening.

—MARY WANLESS, *FOR THE GOOD OF THE HORSE*

•

You know, you didn't get into riding because you were looking for more stress in your life. If you're not enjoying what you're doing, that's your cue to make a change. Don't wait for it to get better; *do* something to make it better. It's so important that you do whatever you can to preserve the sentiment that drew you into riding in the first place.

—JANET SASSON EDGETTE, PSYD, *HEADS UP! PRACTICAL SPORTS PSYCHOLOGY FOR RIDERS, THEIR FAMILIES AND THEIR TRAINERS*

The riding of young horses is an excellent nerve tonic.
—GEOFFREY BROOKE, *TRAINING YOUNG HORSES TO JUMP*

Keep one leg on one side, the other leg on the
other side, and your mind in the middle.
—HENRY TAYLOR, "RIDING LESSON"

A perfect book on riding could be written only by a horse.
—VLADIMIR S. LITTAUER, *COMMON SENSE HORSEMANSHIP*

Out of the West

A cowboy is a man with guts and a horse.

—ATTRIBUTED TO WILL JAMES

He was a picture to make any cowboy miss a few heartbeats as
he sometimes raced across the prairie sod and with head and tail
up showed off the qualities that stuck out at his every move.

—WILL JAMES, *SMOKY THE COWHORSE*

Life is a catch pen full of rodeo broncs, and the way I figure it, forty-six years into this buck-out, the mission is to decide early on, *Did you come to hide, or did you come to ride?*

—PAUL ZARZYSKI, "GOOD HORSEKEEPING," IN
HORSE PEOPLE, EDITED BY MICHAEL J. ROSEN

●

He's cow-smart and brave—though sometimes a clown—
and to the man with sky in his eye and mud on his
boots the Quarter Horse is a faithful hand . . .
And a friend!

—REX CAUBLE, "WHAT IS A QUARTER HORSE,"
QUOTED IN *THE COMPLETE BOOK OF THE AMERICAN
QUARTER HORSE* BY NELSON C. NYE

Oh, when I die, take my saddle from the wall,

Put it on my pony, lead him out of his stall;

Tie my bones to his back, turn our faces to the West,

And we'll ride the prairies that we love best.

—"I RIDE AN OLD PAINT"

When the stranger hit the saddle, Dunny quit the earth,

And traveled right straight up for all that he was worth,

A-pitching and a-squealing and a-having wall-eye fits,

His hind feet perpendicular, his front feet in the bits.

—"ZEBRA DUN"

There never was a horse that couldn't be rode. There

never was a cowboy that couldn't be throwed.

—COWBOY SAYING

In the language of the range, to say that somebody is "as smart as
a cutting horse" is to say that he is smarter than a Philadelphia
lawyer, smarter than a steel trap, smarter than a coyote, smarter
than a Harvard graduate—all combined. There just can't
be anything smarter than a smart cutting horse. He can do
everything but talk Meskin—and he understands that . . .

—JOE M. EVANS, *A CORRAL FULL OF STORIES*

In the Old West the phrase "left afoot" meant nothing short of being left flat on your back. "A man on foot is no man at all," the saying went. If an enemy could not take a man's life, the next best thing was to take his horse.

—J. FRANK DOBIE, *GUIDE TO LIFE AND LITERATURE OF THE SOUTHWEST*

Rodeoing is about the only sport you can't fix. You'd have to talk to the bulls and horses, and they wouldn't understand you.

—BILL LINDERMAN

A cowboy climbed aboard a bronc, which commenced to buck. The bronc threw one particular buck that caused the cowboy to lose his stirrups while, at the same time, the bronc caught a hind leg in one of the stirrups. Whereupon the cowboy went flying out of the saddle. When the onlookers asked the cowboy what had happened, he replied, "well, boys, when I looked down and saw that bronc's foot in the stirrup, I said to myself, 'hell, if he's gettin' on, I'd better get off.'"

—ANONYMOUS

When you're young and you fall off a horse, you may break
something. When you're my age and you fall off, you splatter.

—ROY ROGERS

Never approach a bull from the front, a horse from
the rear or a fool from any direction.

—COWBOY SAYING

The pony saw through it. No feint hoodwinked him. This animal
was thoroughly a man of the world. His undistracted eye stayed
fixed upon the dissembling foe, and the gravity of his horse-
expression made the matter one of high comedy. Then the
rope would sail out at him, but he was already elsewhere; and
if horses laugh, gayety must have abounded in that corral.

—OWEN WISTER, *THE WESTERNER*

May your belly never grumble,

May your heart never ache.

May your horse never stumble,

May your cinch never break.

—COWBOY BLESSING

A good horse is never a bad color.
—COWBOY SAYING

Practice sharpens, but overschooling blunts the edge. If your horse isn't doing right, the first place to look is yourself.
—JOE HEIM, QUOTED IN *CUTTING, ONE RUN AT A TIME* BY BARBRA SCHULTE

When that horse hit the ground I felt as though Saint Peter and all the guards of the Pearly Gates who I'd been to see just a second before, had put their foot down on me and was trying to push me through the earth to the hot place. The saddle horn was tickling me under the chin and one of my feet touched the ground, my other one was alongside the horse's jaw.
—WILL JAMES, *THE DRIFTING COWBOY*

That's a horse to cross rivers on.

—WESTERN EXPRESSION DESCRIBING
A GOOD SWIMMING HORSE

A cowman saddles and unsaddles his own horse,
and an offer to help is unwelcome.

—RAMON ADAMS, *THE COWMAN'S CODE OF ETHICS*

The toughest broncs is them you rode some other place.

—WESTERN SAYING

If you're a cowboy and you're dragging a guy behind
your horse, I bet it would really make you mad if you
looked back and the guy was reading a magazine.

—JACK HANDEY, *DEEP THOUGHTS*

No matter how hungry he may be, [the cowman] takes care
of his horse before looking after his own comfort.

—RAMON ADAMS, *THE COWMAN'S CODE OF ETHICS*

A cutting competition is nothing more than a contest of "oh shits" and "attaboys." And the person with more attaboys is the winner.

—BUSTER WELCH, QUOTED IN *TRAINING AND SHOWING THE CUTTING HORSE* BY LYNN CAMPION

In those border days every rider loved his horse as a part of himself. If there was a difference between any rider of the sage and Bostil, it was, as Bostil had more horses, so had he more love.

—ZANE GREY, "THE HORSES OF BOSTIL'S FORD"

I once gave Eugen Herrigel's little masterpiece *Zen in the Art of Archery* to Buster [Welch, the cutting-horse trainer] to read and he concluded that its application to horsemanship was that if you are thinking about your riding, you are interfering with your horse.

—THOMAS McGUANE, "BUSTER," *SOME HORSES*

Halted in animated expectancy or running in abandoned freedom,
the mustang was the most beautiful, the most spirited and the most
inspiring creature ever to print foot on the grasses of America.

—J. FRANK DOBIE, *THE MUSTANGS*

When I was doctor'n' a horse, the story would come up about what
he had done and who he had saved and they'd say, "Save him if you
can!" Nobody in the ranch country ever insulted a good horse by
talking about what it would cost to replace him and the telephone
operators whose help was indispensable in this particular epidemic
were mostly all girls and women with ranch background or who
were married to a cowboy and the general thought in treating
horses was never about money but instead was to save the horse
for the good he had done or for what he meant to somebody.

—BEN K. GREEN, *THE VILLAGE HORSE
DOCTOR: WEST OF THE PECOS*

A Shakespearean Interlude

Certainly the most widely known equestrian quotation in the English language comes from William Shakespeare's historical play *Richard III*:

A horse! A horse! My kingdom for a horse!
— *RICHARD III*, ACT 5, SCENE 4

[However, the Bard's plays and poetry contain many more references to horses and horsemanship. Let's begin with this extended excerpt from "Venus and Adonis":]

But lo! from forth a copse that neighbours by,
Abreeding jennet, lusty, young, and proud,
Adonis' tramping courier doth espy,
And forth she rushes, snorts and neighs aloud:
The strong-neck'd steed, being tied unto a tree,
Breaketh his rein, and to her straight goes he.

Imperiously he leaps, he neighs, he bounds,
And now his woven girths he breaks asunder;
The bearing earth with his hard hoof he wounds,
Whose hollow womb resounds like heaven's thunder;
The iron bit he crusheth 'tween his teeth,
Controlling what he was controlled with.

His ears up-prick'd; his braided hanging mane
Upon his compass'd crest now stand on end;
His nostrils drink the air, and forth again,
As from a furnace, vapours doth he send:
His eye, which scornfully glisters like fire,
Shows his hot courage and his high desire.

Sometime he trots, as if he told the steps,
With gentle majesty and modest pride;
Anon he rears upright, curvets and leaps,
As who should say, "Lo! thus my strength is tried;
And this I do to captivate the eye
Of the fair breeder that is standing by."

What recketh he his rider's angry stir,
His flattering "Holla," or his "Stand, I say"?
What cares he now for curb or pricking spur?
For rich caparisons or trapping gay?
He sees his love, and nothing else he sees,
Nor nothing else with his proud sight agrees.

Look, when a painter would surpass the life,
In limning out a well-proportion'd steed,
His art with nature's workmanship at strife,
As if the dead the living should exceed;
So did this horse excel a common one,
In shape, in courage, colour, pace and bone.

Round-hoof'd, short-jointed, fetlocks shag and long,
Broad breast, full eye, small head, and nostril wide,
High crest, short ears, straight legs and passing strong,
Thin mane, thick tail, broad buttock, tender hide:
Look, what a horse should have he did not lack,
Save a proud rider on so proud a back.

—"VENUS AND ADONIS," LINES 259–300

[In the following exchange, Richard II, imprisoned after
Henry Bolingbroke usurped the throne, is told by a
groom that Brolingbroke rode the king's horse, Barbary,
to Bolingbroke's coronation as King Henry IV:]

King Richard: Rode he on Barbary? Tell me, gentle friend,
How went he under him?
Groom: So proudly as if he disdain'd the ground.
King Richard: So proud that Bolingbroke was on his back!
That jade hath eat bread from my royal hand;
This hand hath made him proud with clapping him.
Would he not stumble? Would he not fall down,
Since pride must have a fall, and break the neck
Of that proud man that did usurp his back?
Forgiveness, horse! Why do I rail on thee,
Since thou, created to be aw'd by man,
Wast born to bear? I was not made a horse;
And yet I bear a burden like an ass,
Spurr'd, gall'd and tir'd, by jauncing Bolingbroke.

—RICHARD II, ACT 5, SCENE 5

But hollow men, like horses hot at hand,

Make gallant show and promise of their mettle;

But when they should endure the bloody spur,

They fall their crests, and like deceitful jades,

Sink in the trial.

—*JULIUS CAESAR*, ACT 4, SCENE 2

Young hot colts being raged do rage the more.

—*RICHARD II*, ACT 2, SCENE 1

Like unback'd colts, they prick'd their ears,

Advanced their eyelids, lifted up their noses

As they smelled music.

—*THE TEMPEST*, ACT 4, SCENE 1

I wish your horses swift and sure of foot;

And so I do command you to their backs.

—MACBETH, ACT 3, SCENE 1

He doth nothing but talk of his horse.

—THE MERCHANT OF VENICE, ACT 1, SCENE 2

Rise from the ground like feather'd Mercury,

And vaulted with such ease into his seat

As if an angel dropp'd down from the clouds,

To turn and wind a fiery Pegasus

And witch the world with noble horsemanship.

—HENRY IV, PART 1, ACT 4, SCENE 1

I will not change my horse with any that treads on four pasterns. Ca, ha! He bounds from the earth, as if his entrails were hairs, le cheval volant, the Pegasus, chez les narines de feu! When I bestride him, I soar, I am a hawk: he trots the air; the earth sings when he touches it; the basest horn of his hoof is more musical than the pipe of Hermes . . . He is pure air and fire . . . The prince of palfreys; his neigh is like the bidding of a monarch and his countenance enforces homage.

—*HENRY V, ACT 3, SCENE 7*

Those that tame wild horses

Pace 'em not in their hands to make 'em gentle,

But stop their mouths with stubborn bits, and spur 'em

Till they obey the manage.

—*HENRY VIII*, ACT 5, SCENE 3

Beggars mounted run their horses to death.

—*HENRY VI*, PART 3, ACT 1, SCENE 4 [SIMILAR TO
"SET A BEGGAR ON HORSEBACK AND HE WILL RIDE A
GALLOP" (ROBERT BURTON, *ANATOMY OF MELANCHOLY*)
AND THE GERMAN PROVERB, "SET A BEGGAR ON
HORSEBACK, AND HE'LL OUTRIDE THE DEVIL."]

Well could he ride, and often men would say

"That horse his mettle from his rider takes:

Proud of subjection, noble by the sway,

What rounds, what bounds, what course, what stop he makes!"

And controversy hence a question takes,

Whether the horse by him became his deed,

Or he his manage by the well-doing steed.

—"A LOVER'S COMPLAINT," LINES 106–12

What a piece of work is a horse! How noble in reason! How infinite in faculty! In form and moving how express and admirable! In action how like an angel! In apprehension how like a man! The beauty of the world! The paragon of animals!

—JAMES AGATE, *ALARUMS AND EXCURSIONS* [MODELED ON *HAMLET*'S "WHAT A PIECE OF WORK MAN IS!" SPEECH]

■ ■ ■ ■ ■ ■ ■ ■ ■

Racing—The Sport of Kings

[Neptune] created the horse and was the patron of horse races.

His own horses had brazen hooves and golden manes.

—BULFINCH'S MYTHOLOGY, "NEPTUNE"

●

The utter joy of riding Template lay in the immense power which he generated. There was no need to make the best of things, on his back; to fiddle and scramble, and to hope for others to blunder, and find nothing to spare for a finish. He had enough reserve strength for his jockey to be able to carve up the race as he wished, and there was nothing in racing, I thought, more ecstatic than that.

—DICK FRANCIS, *NERVE*

When you peel back the layers of racing, you
are left with the horse and the groom.
—TRAINER AND TV COMMENTATOR CHARLSIE CANTEY,
QUOTED IN *THE BACKSTRETCH* MAGAZINE

Horse racing is the sport of kings and the trap of fools.
—ANONYMOUS

It is not best that we all think alike; it is difference
of opinion that makes horse races.
—MARK TWAIN, *PUDD'NHEAD WILSON*

Too much hope is perhaps the worst sin in horse racing.

—SIMON BARNES, "TALKING HORSES,"
IN THE *TIMES* (LONDON)

●

A horse gallops with his lungs, preserves with
his heart, and wins with his character.

—FEDERICO TESIO, *BREEDING THE RACEHORSE*

●

The harrowing uncertainty of the turf.

—SPORTS COLUMNIST AND AUTHOR RED SMITH

As some swift horse

Is reined in by his rider, when he strains

Unto the race-course, and he neighs, and champs

The curbing bit, dashing his chest with foam,

And his feet eager for the course are still

Never, his restless hooves are clattering aye;

His mane is a stormy cloud, he tosses high

His head with snortings, and his lord is glad . . .

—QUINTUS SMYRNAEUS, *THE FALL OF TROY*

The race is not always to the swift nor the battle

to the strong—but that's the way to bet.

—DAMON RUNYAN, *MORE THAN SOMEWHAT*

Horses have never hurt anyone yet, except when they bet on them.

—STUART CLOETE, *THE HONEY BIRD*
AND OTHER AFRICAN STORIES

I'll be around as long as horses think I'm smarter than they are.

—TRAINER JAMES E. "SUNNY JIM" FITZSIMMONS
[WHO CONTINUED TO TRAIN HORSES INTO HIS NINETIES]

Now a barrier looms, dark and menacing, in your path. You feel
an almost imperceptible change in your horse's momentum as he
adjusts his stride to meet the takeoff point. You tighten your legs
against his sides to give encouragement in the last few critical
strides. Your body picks up the horse's emphatic rhythm, and you
feel the great hindquarters gather under you. Suddenly, you are
in the air, feeling the clean, exhilarating sensation of a flight.

You are on a 'chaser.

—RAYMOND WOOLFE JR., *STEEPLECHASING*

Morning glory.

**—RACETRACK EXPRESSION FOR A HORSE THAT
TURNS IN IMPRESSIVE MORNING WORKOUTS,
BUT FAILS TO WIN IN THE AFTERNOON**

•

A racehorse is an animal that can take several
thousand people for a ride at the same time.

—ANONYMOUS

•

You can take an old mule and run him and feed him
and train him and get him in the best shape of his life,
but you ain't going to win the Kentucky Derby!

—SOUTHERN PROVERB

And such running! It was rather the long leaping of lions in harness;
but for the lumbering chariot, it seemed the four were flying.

—LEW WALLACE, *BEN-HUR*

●

The Perfect Horseman is quiet on a horse. The calmness
which springs from confidence in his own ability extends to
the horse and quietens him too. Nothing frightens a horse as
much as a frightened rider, and nothing will make a horse more
restless and fidgety than a rider who cannot sit still . . .
Everyone realizes that a bad rider can make a thoroughbred look like
a cart-horse, but unless a horse is fleet of foot the Perfect Horseman
and the Perfect Jockey rolled into one cannot win races on him. The
jockey is there to guide, help, drive, cajole, or even coax his horse
into the winner's enclosure, but he cannot go faster than the horse.

—DICK FRANCIS, *THE SPORT OF QUEENS*

If you've never been crazy about thoroughbreds it's because you've never been around where they are much and don't know any better. They're beautiful. There isn't anything so lovely and clean and full of spunk and honesty and everything as some racehorses.

—SHERWOOD ANDERSON, "I WANT TO KNOW WHY"

I was nuts about the horses, too. There's something about it, when they come out and go up the track to the post. Sort of dancy and tight looking with the jock keeping a tight hold on them and maybe easing off a little and letting them run a little going up.

—ERNEST HEMINGWAY, "MY OLD MAN"

The sunshine's golden gleam is thrown

On sorrel, chestnut, bay and roan;

The horses prance and paw and neigh,

Fillies and colts like kittens play,

And dance and toss their rippled manes

Shining and soft as silken skeins.

—OLIVER WENDELL HOLMES SR.,
"HOW THE OLD HORSE WON THE BET"

"Races are won with that seat, sir."

"Be damned to that," said my uncle Valentine. "If the horse
is good enough, he'll win with the rider facing his tail."

—DOROTHEA DONN BYRNE, "DESTINY BAY"

The little bright mare, made of nerves and steel springs,

Shot level beside him, shot ahead as with wings.

Charles felt his horse quicken, felt the desperate beat

Of the blood in his body from his knees to his feet.

—JOHN MASEFIELD, *RIGHT ROYAL*

There are a hundred ways to lose a race, but only one way to win one.

— RACING MAXIM

A racetrack is a place where the human race is secondary.

— ANONYMOUS

Most good horses know when they'd won: filled their lungs and raised their heads with pride. Some were definitely depressed when they lost. Guilt they never felt, nor shame nor regret nor compassion.

— DICK FRANCIS, *BREAK IN*

Horse sense is the thing a horse has which keeps it from betting on people.

— W. C. FIELDS

Here is living harmony in horseflesh; an embodiment
of rhythm and modulation, of point and counterpoint,
that sang to the eye and made music in the heart.

—JOHN HERVEY [SALVADORE] ON THE
GREAT RACEHORSE EQUIPOISE

He was as near living flame as horses ever get.

—JOE PALMER ON MAN O' WAR

The heart is like a race horse on a plain, easy to let go, hard to rein in.

—CHINESE PROVERB

The blood runs hot in the Thoroughbred and the courage runs
deep. In the best of them, pride is limitless. This is their heritage
and they carry it like a banner. What they have, they use.

—C. W. ANDERSON

The fires burnt high in him. He should have lived with the wild horses of the prairie where he could have been boss. There the issue would have been settled quickly; he would have ruled or died. But civilization got him instead. Man laid hold of his bridle. "All right," said Display, "you asked for it," and he gave it to them. Finally he did what they asked but not because he had changed his mind.

—J. A. ESTES, ON THE THOROUGHBRED RACEHORSE DISPLAY

Horses and jockeys mature earlier than people—which is why horses are admitted to racetracks at the age of two, and jockeys before they are old enough to shave.

—DICK BEDDOES

Don't fall off.

—ADVICE GIVEN BY HOLLIE HUGHES, AN ELDERLY
TRAINER, TO SECRETARIAT'S JOCKEY RON TURCOTTE
BEFORE THE 1973 BELMONT STAKES (WHICH SECRETARIAT
WENT ON TO WIN BY THIRTY-THREE LENGTHS)

Out on the Texas plains a fellow had to be a smart horseman to
win a race and a smarter one to win a bet—and collect it!

—SAMUEL CLAY HILDRETH, *THE SPELL OF THE
TURF*, QUOTED IN *THE COLONIAL QUARTER RACE
HORSE* BY ALEXANDER MACKAY-SMITH

There appears to be no immunity to this dangerous germ. If as a
parent you observe your little precious pick up a toy horse, make
galloping noises, and plop it over a block, screaming "Win!"
you've had it. The jumping rider's disease is loose in your house.

—RAYMOND WOOLFE JR., *STEEPLECHASING*

A trainer can always find an excuse for a defeat, whether it's a
mistake in judgment by the jockey or the conditions of the track or
a bit of poor racing luck. Maybe just a little adjustment—a new rider
or a change in equipment or a different post position—will make
the next outcome different. "This is the great thing about racing,"
trainer D. Wayne Lucas once said. "There's always another race."

—BILLY REED, *THOROUGHBRED: A CELEBRATION OF THE BREED*

■ ■ ■ ■ ■ ■ ■ ■ ■

A Pack of Hunting Quotations

It ain't the 'unting as 'urts 'un, it's the 'ammer,

'ammer, 'ammer along the 'ard, 'igh ground.

—*PUNCH* MAGAZINE CARTOON CAPTION

There are only two classes of good society in England; the

equestrian classes and the neurotic classes. It isn't mere

convention; everybody can see that the people who hunt are the

right people and the people who don't are the wrong ones.

—GEORGE BERNARD SHAW, *HEARTBREAK HOUSE*

Old John had brought his Whips [whippers-in], all five of them still mounted like himself and fresh from the hunt, clomping into the grand salon to admire Whistlejacket, one of the finest portraits of a horse ever painted by George Stubbs. The horses of the five Whips trod on polished floors and French floor coverings, the men said down to a man that looking at Whistlejacket from the saddle gave a new and admirable perspective to the grandeur of the horse, no matter that several of the living horses shied from the painted animal or attempted to rear up in imitation of it. This event sent Great-Grandmother to her bed for a week.

—JOHN HAWKES, *WHISTLEJACKET*

With the Meadowbrook Hunt they were always in front,

And fearless of all disaster.

Over bar and gate they would lead on straight.

Old Mohawk—and his Master.

—ANONYMOUS QUATRAIN IN HONOR OF ELLIOTT ROOSEVELT,
MASTER OF THE MEADOWBROOK HUNT ON LONG ISLAND,
NEW YORK, AND HIS HORSE, OLD MOHAWK [ROOSEVELT
WAS THE FATHER OF FIRST LADY ELEANOR ROOSEVELT.]

Today, all day, I rode upon the down,

With hounds and horsemen, a brave company . . .

And once, when check'd, a thrush sang, and my horse

Prick'd his quick ears as to a sound unknown.

. . . Your face my quarry was. For it I rode,

My horse a thing of wings, myself a god.

—WILFRID SCAWEN BLUNT, "ST. VALENTINE'S DAY"

'Aving the 'ead of a dutchess and the arse of a cook.

—ENGLISH DESCRIPTION OF AN IDEAL HUNTING HORSE

The horses snort to be at the sport,

The dogs are running free;

The woods rejoice at the merry noise

Of hey taranta tee ree.

—WILLIAM GRAY, "THE KING'S HUNT IS UP"

The first Marchioness [of Salisbury] was painted by Sir
Joshua Reynolds, and hunted till the day she died at eighty-
five, when, half-blind and strapped to the saddle, she was
accompanied by a groom who would shout, when her horse
approached a fence, "Jump, dammit, my Lady, jump!"

—BARBARA TUCHMAN, THE PROUD TOWER

Three jolly gentlemen

Dressed in red

Rode their horses

Up to bed.

—WALTER DE LA MARE, "THE HUNTSMEN"

●

Remember that the most important gait of the hunter is the halt.

—WILLIAM P. WADSWORTH, MFH, *RIDING TO HOUNDS*
IN AMERICA: AN INTRODUCTION FOR FOXHUNTERS

"Black" ditches are full of dark murky water, the color of
Guinness stout but hardly so tasty. Waiting your turn, watching
horses and rider in front scrambling up the bank, only to
slide back into the ditch and emerge, covered with black
murky water, you ask yourself, Why am I doing this?

—JOY SLATER, WITH STEVEN D. PRICE, *RIDING'S A JOY*

The English gentleman galloping after a fox—the
unspeakable in full pursuit of the uneatable.

—OSCAR WILDE, *A WOMAN OF NO IMPORTANCE*

Horse Laughs

I never play horseshoes 'cause Mother taught

us not to throw our clothes around.

—MR. ED [THE "TALKING HORSE" OF THE 1960S TV SERIES]

Paying alimony is like feeding hay to a dead horse.

—ATTRIBUTED TO GROUCHO MARX

If the world was truly a rational place, men would ride sidesaddle.

—RITA MAE BROWN

I once bet on a horse that was so slow, I bet it to live.

I played a great horse yesterday! It took seven horses to beat him.

The horse I bet on was so slow, the jockey kept a diary of the trip.

My horse's jockey was hitting the horse. The horse turns around
and says, "Why are you hitting me, there is nobody behind us!"

That was the first time I saw a horse start from a kneeling position!

My horse was so late getting home, he tiptoed into the stable.

I don't mind when my horse is left at the post. I don't mind
when my horse comes up to me in the stands and asks,
"Which way do I go?" But when the horse I bet on is at the
$2 window betting on another horse in the same race . . .

—HENNY YOUNGMAN

Horse crazy. It happens to a lot of little girls. I think my case was fairly modest considering the more virulent strains of this epizootic. When I watched cowboy movies (and God knows I'm still a sucker for a Republic Western), it was the horse that held me in thrall. And while I had guns and holsters aplenty, my interest wasn't in the gunfight at the OK Corral, but riding off into the sunset on Topper, or Champion, or Trigger. Tarzan, Diablo, or Silver.

—CANDYCE BARNES, "BOOTS, SADDLE, TO HOME, AND AWAY," IN *HORSE PEOPLE*, EDITED BY MICHAEL J. ROSEN [TOPPER, CHAMPION, TRIGGER, TARZAN, DIABLO, AND SILVER WERE THE HORSES OF COWBOY MOVIE HEROES HOPALONG CASSIDY, GENE AUTRY, ROY ROGERS, KEN MAYNARD, THE CISCO KID, AND THE LONE RANGER, RESPECTIVELY.]

My experience of horses is that they never throw away a chance to go lame, and that in all respects they are well meaning and unreliable animals. I have also observed that if you refuse a high price for a favorite horse, he will go and lay down somewhere and die.

—MARK TWAIN, IN THE *SAN FRANCISCO BULLETIN*

I know the horse too well. I have known the horse in war and in peace, and there is no place where a horse is comfortable. A horse thinks of too many things to do which you do not expect. He is apt to bite you in the leg when you think he is half asleep. The horse has too many caprices, and he is too much given to initiative. He invents too many new ideas. No, I don't want anything to do with a horse.

—MARK TWAIN, *SPEECHES*

I am not an expert in horses and do not speak with assurance. I can always tell which is the front end of a horse, but beyond that, my art is not above the ordinary.

—MARK TWAIN, *A BIOGRAPHY*

If the horses knew their strength we should not ride anymore.

—MARK TWAIN, NOTEBOOK #42

I realize that the concept of wild horses probably stirs romantic notions in many of you, but this is because you have never met any wild horses in person. In person, they are like enormous hooved rats. They amble up to your camp site, and their attitude is: "We're wild horses. We're going to eat your food, knock down your tent and poop on your shoes. We're protected by federal law, just like Richard Nixon."

—DAVE BARRY, "TENTING GRANDPA BOB"

There you are, $600,000 on four hooves. I bet a Russian Czar never paid that kind of dough for a single horse.

—*THE GODFATHER* [FILM VERSION, 1972, SCREENPLAY BY FRANCIS FORD COPPOLA]

My dear, I don't care what they do, so long as they
don't do it in the street and frighten the horses.

—MRS. PATRICK CAMPBELL, ENGLISH ACTRESS
OF THE EARLY TWENTIETH CENTURY

Certain comic effects can be achieved by a brand-new rider, especially
a man who dresses like a fashion model and rides like a tailor.

—C. J. J. MULLEN, *LIFE ON A SLIGHTLY USED HORSE*

I've spent most of my life riding horses. The rest I've just wasted.

—ANONYMOUS

●

In what other sport do you put on leather boots, stretch-fabric breeches, a shirt and tie, a wool jacket, a velvet-covered cap, and leather gloves, and *then* go out and exercise?

—A. LONDON WOLF [ON HORSE SHOWING IN NINETY-PLUS-DEGREE SUMMER WEATHER]

I ride horses because it's the only sport where
I can exercise while sitting down.
— JOAN HANSEN

Horses do think. Not very deeply, perhaps, but
enough to get you into a lot of trouble.
— PATRICIA JACOBSON AND MARCIA HAYES,
A HORSE AROUND THE HOUSE

Anyone who is concerned about his dignity would
be well advised to keep away from horses.
— PRINCE PHILIP, DUKE OF EDINBURGH

People on horses look better than they are.

People in cars look worse than they are.

—MARYA MANNES

People on horses look better than they are.

Look, Mommy, he's wearing bell-bottoms!

—SMALL CHILD'S REACTION TO SEEING A CLYDESDALE'S FETLOCK "FEATHERS"

Riding: The art of keeping a horse between you and the ground.

—ANONYMOUS

Speak kindly to your little horse,

And soothe him when he wheezes,

Or he may turn his back on you,

And kick you where he pleases.

—ANONYMOUS

The daughter who won't lift a finger in the house is

the same child who cycles madly off in the pouring

rain to spend all morning mucking out a stable.

—SAMANTHA ARMSTRONG

A horse is dangerous at both ends and uncomfortable in the middle.

—IAN FLEMING, QUOTED IN THE SUNDAY
TIMES (LONDON), OCTOBER 9, 1966

Want to end up with a million bucks in the horse
business? Start out with five million.

—ANONYMOUS

To confess that you are totally ignorant about the horse is social
suicide: you will be despised by everybody, especially the horse.

—W. C. SELLAR, *HORSE NONSENSE*

How do you catch a loose horse? Make a noise like a carrot.
—BRITISH CAVALRY JOKE

I prefer a bike to a horse. The brakes are more easily checked.
—LAMBERT JEFFRIES

You can lead a horse to water, but if you can teach him to roll over and float on his back, then you got something.
—JOE E. LEWIS

Horse Truths

And God took a handful of southerly wind, blew
his breath over it and created the horse.

—BEDOUIN LEGEND

Time is the rider that breaks youth.

—GEORGE HERBERT, *JACULA PRUDENTUM*

He that will venture nothing must not get on horse-back.

—C. J. APPERLEY [NIMROD], *QUARTERLY REVIEW*

A prince is never surrounded by as much majesty

on his throne as he is on a beautiful horse.

—WILLIAM CAVENDISH, DUKE OF NEWCASTLE, *A GENERAL*

SYSTEM OF HORSEMANSHIP IN ALL ITS BRANCHES

The true character of the horse is never completely revealed in the stable or in the riding school, beneath the saddle or in harness. To know him as he really is we must watch him under the open sky, in the meadow, among his own kind, for there we can see how different each horse is from his companions, how the ancient law of the herd lives on, and how the hierarchy is created with barely an encounter.

—HANS-HEINRICH ISENBART, *THE BEAUTY OF THE HORSE*

An owner [of a Tennessee walking horse] once said that his
horse reminded him of a lightning rod, for, as he rode, all
the sorrows of his heart flowed down through the splendid
muscles of his horse and were grounded in the earth.

—MARGUERITE HENRY, *ALBUM OF HORSES*

For many of us, the horse is a symbol of what is right with the world.
In spite of generations of careful breeding, the horse still seems to be
a step or two out of the wild. In spite of training and confinement,
the horse at gallop seems to be a step or two from freedom.

—SHARON B. SMITH, *THE AFFORDABLE HORSE*

God forbid that I should go to any heaven in which there are no horses.

—R. B. CUNNINGHAME GRAHAM, IN A LETTER
TO PRESIDENT THEODORE ROOSEVELT

It is not enough for a man to know how to
ride; he must know how to fall.

—MEXICAN PROVERB

There is something about the outside of a horse
that is good for the inside of a man.

—SIR WINSTON CHURCHILL [ALSO ATTRIBUTED TO
ANOTHER BRITISH PRIME MINISTER, LORD PALMERSTON.
WHEN THIS QUOTE ONCE APPEARED IN *THE CHRONICLE
OF THE HORSE* MAGAZINE, IT HAD THE FOLLOWING
TYPO: THERE IS SOMETHING ABOUT THE OUTSIDE OF A
HORSE THAT IS GOOD FOR THE INSIDE OF A MARE.]

Many people have sighed for the "good old days" and regretted
the "passing of the horse," but today, when only those who
like horses own them, it is a far better time for horses.

—C. W. ANDERSON, *THE COMPLETE BOOK
OF HORSES AND HORSEMANSHIP*

The wagon rests in winter, the sleigh in summer, the horse never.

—YIDDISH PROVERB

●

No ride is ever the last one. No horse is ever the last one you will have. Somehow there will always be other horses, other places to ride them.

—MONICA DICKENS, *TALKING OF HORSES*

●

The horse is God's gift to man.

—ARABIAN PROVERB

Show me your horse and I will tell you who you are.

—ENGLISH PROVERB

Dog lovers hate to clean out kennels. Horse lovers like cleaning stables.

—MONICA DICKENS, *TALKING OF HORSES*

To ride a horse well, you have to know it as
well as you know your best friend.

—GRAND PRIX SHOW-JUMPING RIDER KATIE MONAHAN
PRUDENT, IN A ROLEX ADVERTISEMENT

●

There is no secret so close as that between a rider and his horse.

—ROBERT SMITH SURTEES, *MR. SPONGE'S SPORTING TOUR*

●

Nothing on four legs is quicker than a horse heading back to the barn.

—PAMELA C. BIDDLE AND JOEL E. FISHMAN,
ALL I NEED TO KNOW I LEARNED FROM MY HORSE

The ears never lie.

— DON BURT

You will find it is always easier to walk if
there is a horse between your legs.

— ANONYMOUS

When the horse's jaws are in motion, his mind is at rest.

— PETE ROSE

Horses leave hoofprints on your heart.

— ANONYMOUS

A horse is a thing of such beauty . . . none will tire of looking at him as long as he displays himself in his splendor.

—XENOPHON, *ON HORSEMANSHIP*

God first made Man. He thought better of it and made Woman. When He got time He made the Horse, which has the courage and spirit of Man and the beauty and grace of Woman.

—BRAZILIAN SAYING

The air of heaven is that which blows between a horse's ears.

—ARABIAN PROVERB

This most noble beast is the most beautiful, the swiftest and of
the highest courage of domesticated animals. His long mane
and tail adorn and beautify him. He is of a fiery temperament,
but good tempered, obedient, docile and well-mannered.

—PEDRO GARCÍA CONDE, 1685

We have almost forgotten how strange a thing it is that so huge and powerful and intelligent an animal as a horse should allow another, and far more feeble animal, to ride upon its back.

—PETER GRAY

Speak your mind, but ride a fast horse.

—ANONYMOUS

Horses change lives. They give our young people confidence and self-esteem. They provide peace and tranquility to troubled souls—they give us hope!

—TONI ROBINSON

A Hibernian sage once wrote that there are three things a man never forgets: The girl of his early youth, a devoted teacher, and a great horse.

—C. J. J. MULLEN

●

The horse through all its trials has preserved
the sweetness of paradise in its blood.

—JOHANNES JENSEN

We gaze upon their quiet beauty, their natural elegance, and we are captivated. They see us softly, in gentle light . . . rewarding human companionship with strength, grace and intelligence. As they run through arenas and open fields, past mountains and seas, moving like the wind toward heaven, we travel with them, if only in our hearts.

—ANONYMOUS

Wherever man has left his footprint in the long ascent from barbarism to civilization, we will find the hoofprint of a horse beside it.

—JOHN TROTWOOD MOORE

Look back on our struggle for freedom,

Trace our present day strength to its source,

And you'll find that man's pathway to glory,

Is strewn with the bones of a horse.

—ANONYMOUS

Never give up. For fifty years they said the horse was

through. Now look at him—a status symbol.

—FLETCHER KNEBEL

The wind flew. God told the wind to condense itself
and out of the flurry came the horse. But with the
spark of spirit the horse flew by the wind itself.

—MARGUERITE HENRY, *KING OF THE WIND*

A horse already knows how to be a horse; the rider has to
learn how to become a rider. A horse without a rider is still
a horse; a rider without a horse is no longer a rider.

—ANONYMOUS

To be loved by a horse, or by any animal, should fill

us with awe—for we have not deserved it.

—MARION GARRETTY

A horse loves freedom, and the weariest old work

horse will roll on the ground or break into a lumbering

gallop when he is turned loose into the open.

—GERALD RAFTERY

My horse has a hoof of striped agate. His fetlock is like fine

eagle plume. His legs are like quick lightning. My horse

has a tail like a trailing black cloud. His mane is made of

short rainbows. My horse's eyes are made of big stars.

—NAVAJO WAR GOD'S HORSE SONG

The horse is a creature who sacrifices his own being to exist through the will of another . . . he is the noble conquest of man.

—GEORGES-LOUIS LECLERC, COMTE DE BUFFON

No one can teach riding so well as a horse.

—C. S. LEWIS, *THE HORSE AND HIS BOY*

My horses are my friends, not my slaves.

—DR. REINER KLIMKE

There are times when you can trust a horse, times
when you can't, and times when you have to.

—ANONYMOUS

●

An old friend is like a saddled horse.

—AFGHAN PROVERB

●

As old wood is best to burn; old horses to ride; old books to
read; old wine to drink; so are old friends most trusty to use.

—LEONARD WRIGHT

●

The horses of hope gallop, but the asses of experience go slowly.

—RUSSIAN PROVERB

One must plow with the horses one has.

—GERMAN PROVERB

What the colt learns in youth he continues in old age.

—FRENCH PROVERB

Care, and not fine stables, makes a good horse.

—DANISH PROVERB

Who buys a horse buys care.

—SPANISH PROVERB

A little neglect may breed mischief: for want of a nail
the shoe was lost; for want of a shoe the horse was
lost; and for want of a horse the rider was lost.

—BENJAMIN FRANKLIN, *POOR RICHARD'S ALMANACK* [ALSO
FOUND IN *JACULA PRUDENTUM* BY GEORGE HERBERT]

If you ride a horse, sit close and tight,
If you ride a man, sit easy and light.

—BENJAMIN FRANKLIN

He that riseth late, must trot all day, and shall
scarce overtake his business at night.

—BENJAMIN FRANKLIN, *POOR RICHARD'S ALMANACK*

The child who is fortunate enough to be associated with horses during his formative years can look back on fond memories, and those who continue to ride, hunt, or show during their lifetime seldom experience anything more gratifying than the thrill of winning their first ribbon.

—STEPHEN O. HAWKINS, IN *LEARNING TO RIDE, HUNT, AND SHOW* BY GORDON WRIGHT

●

While there are many things you can fake through in this life, pretending that you know horses when you don't isn't one of them.

—COOKY McCLUNG, *HORSEFOLK ARE DIFFERENT*

The horse loves his oats more than his saddle.

—RUSSIAN PROVERB

Of all creatures, the horse is the noblest.

—GERVASE MARKHAM, *THE COMPLEAT HORSEMAN*

For the student there is, in its season, no better place than the saddle.

—FRANCIS PARKMAN, *AUTOBIOGRAPHY*

Fat is the best color.

—HORSEMAN'S ADAGE

You sometimes hear the old saying "Fat is the best color." This means, of course, that fat covers a multitude of conformation faults and therefore *looks* good—especially to the less discerning horseman.

—ELEANOR F. PRINCE AND GAYDELL M.
COLLIER, *BASIC HORSE CARE*

●

Watching a seasoned pony carry its young rider, one senses the pony is doing the teaching. With an uncanny sense of the rider's limitations and often genuine kindness, ponies seem to possess an intelligence you don't always see in horses.

—NINA DURAN, *A PONY RIDER'S DIARY*

Human reason is like a drunken man on horseback; set
it up on one side and it tumbles over on the other.

—MARTIN LUTHER

Not the fastest horse can catch a word spoken in anger.

—CHINESE PROVERB

Of all creatures God made at the Creation, there is none except
man more excellent, or so much to be respected as a horse.

—BEDOUIN LEGEND

A good horse makes short miles.

—ENGLISH PROVERB

A nod is as good as a wink to a blind horse.

—IRISH PROVERB

[The horse possesses] a singular body and a noble spirit, the principle thereof is a loving and dutiful inclination to the service of Man, wherein he never faileth in Peace nor War . . . and therefore . . . we must needs account it the most noble and necessary of all four-footed Beasts.

—EDWARD TOPSELL, QUOTED IN
HORSEWATCHING BY DESMOND MORRIS

To be an equestrian in the classical sense is not to be just a rider. It is a position in life. It is a stance we take in relation to life. We must make a choice between self-love, the promotion of our own well-being of our ego, and love for the horse. That is the fundamental attitudinal decision that earned Xenophon the title Father of Classical Dressage: he dared to love a horse!

—CHARLES DE KUNFFY, *TRAINING STRATEGIES FOR DRESSAGE RIDERS*

Never threaten to take away a kid's horse, unless you don't care if they start trusting horses more than you. If a young person is having or causing trouble, the horse may be their salvation.

—LESLI K. GROVES, "KIDS & HORSES: RATED PG-17," IN *AMERICA'S HORSE* MAGAZINE

Don't ride the high horse. The fall, when it comes, is hard.

—AMERICAN PROVERB

Soft grass for an old horse.

—BULGARIAN PROVERB

My horse be swift in flight even like a bird,

My horse be swift in flight.

Bear me now in safety far from the enemy's arrows.

And you shall be rewarded with streamers and ribbons red.

—SIOUX WARRIOR'S SONG TO HIS HORSE

Love means attention, which means looking after the

things we love. We call it stable management.

—GEORGE H. MORRIS, *THE AMERICAN JUMPING STYLE*

The horse that pulls the most is usually given the least amount of oats.

—GERMAN PROVERB

There on the tips of fair fresh flowers feedeth

he; how joyous is his neigh,

There, in the midst of sacred pollen hidden,

all is he; how joyous is his neigh.

—NAVAJO SONG

One reason why birds and horses are not unhappy is because
they are not trying to impress other birds and horses.

—DALE CARNEGIE, *HOW TO WIN FRIENDS
AND INFLUENCE PEOPLE*

●

With horses and warriors, you can't judge from their appearance.

—JAPANESE PROVERB

●

No horseman or horsewoman has ever finished learning.

—MARY GORDON-WATSON, *THE HANDBOOK OF RIDING*

●

A wise horse cares not how fast a man may run.

—ARMENIAN PROVERB

If the horse is good, you don't mind paying the rental fee.

—JAPANESE PROVERB

Old horses for young riders, old riders for young horses.

—HORSEMAN'S PROVERB

Nature will never disclose all her secrets to us, and the horse will forever have in store for us novelties, surprises, springing from life itself.

—GEN. ALEXIS L'HOTTE, *QUESTIONS EQUESTRES*, QUOTED IN *EQUITATION: LEARNING AND TEACHING* BY JEAN FROISSARD

Horses are karmic and they come to us in our lives
karmically, when it is time for us truly to learn.

—DOMINIQUE BARBIER, WITH MARY DANIELS,
DRESSAGE FOR THE NEW AGE

●

In order to go fast, one must go slow.

—OLD HORSEMAN'S PROVERB

There is a natural affinity between women and horses, something so basic it creates an immediate foundation for a relationship and a launching pad for almost everything we want to do with a horse.

—MARY D. MIDKIFF, *FITNESS, PERFORMANCE AND THE FEMALE EQUESTRIAN*

War is no place for horses.

—BRITISH SHOW-JUMPING RIDER AND HORSE-SHOW ORGANIZER COL. SIR MIKE ANSELL, *SOLDIER ON*

Never change horses in midstream.

—OLD ADAGE [SIMILARLY: NEVER SWAP HORSES CROSSING A STREAM.]

But a horse is a labor of love as well as a responsibility, an aesthetic as well as a dynamic pleasure, something to contemplate as well as to ride.

—SARAH MONTAGUE, IN *A RIDER'S DIARY* BY NINA DURAN

Horses are something to dream about . . . and to wish for;

fun to watch . . . and to make friends with; nice to pat

. . . and great to hug: and, oh, what a joy to ride!

—DOROTHY HENDERSON PINCH, *HAPPY HORSEMANSHIP*

The slow horse reaches the mill.

—IRISH PROVERB

When I hear somebody talk about a horse or a cow being stupid,

I figure it's a sure sign that animal has outfoxed them.

—TOM DORRANCE

Stable thinking is the ability to say "neigh."

—SOURCE UNKNOWN

An old horse finds its way best.

—NORWEGIAN PROVERB

A loose horse will always be found at the barn.

—INDIAN PROVERB

●

You can lead a horse to water . . . if you got a horse.

—ENGLISH PROVERB

●

The first horse to drink doesn't get dirty water.

—NIGERIAN PROVERB

●

There is no greater pleasure than a nice ride
on a nice horse on a beautiful day.

—JUDY RICHTER, *PONY TALK*

The horse is, like man, the most beautiful and
the most miserable of creatures.

—ROSA BONHEUR

Horses have hoofs to carry them over frost and snow; hair, to
protect them from wind and cold. They eat grass and drink
water, and fling up their heels over the campaign. Such is the
real nature of horses. Palatial dwellings are of no use to them.

—CHUANG-TZU

It is not the duty of the horse to be a biofeedback mechanism for yearning humans; yet it is remarkable how consistently people with horses claimed to have learned much about themselves through them. Certainly, the management of a horse will give you a rapid evaluation of your patience, your powers of concentration, and your ability to hold on to delicate ideas for sustained periods of time.

—THOMAS McGUANE, *SOME HORSES*

The primeval instincts of the horse are nowhere more pronounced than in the bond between the mare and her foal, for the maternal instinct is the strongest in nature. It is this instinct that ensures the survival of the species and determines the character of the mare and her attitude toward other horses and toward man.

—HANS-HEINRICH ISENBART, *THE BEAUTY OF THE HORSE*

Men are better when riding, more just and more understanding,
and more alert and more at ease and more under-taking,
and better knowing of all countries and all passages . . .

—EDWARD, SECOND DUKE OF YORK, *THE MASTER OF GAME*

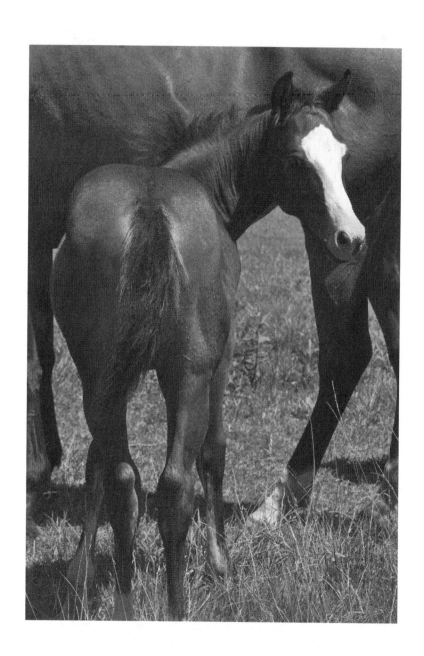

Reason lies between the spur and the bridle.

—GEORGE HERBERT, *JACULA PRUDENTUM*

I have thought that to breed a noble horse is to share with
God in one of His mysteries, as well as one of His delights.

—TOM LEA, *THE HANDS OF CANTU*

A horse is worth more than riches.

—SPANISH PROVERB

INDEX

■ ■ ■ ■ ■ ■ ■ ■ ■ ■